Not ORDINARY LIVES 2

Movers & Shakers
Volume 1

Memoirs of
16 Ordinary People
Doing Extraordinary Things

Peter J Snow OAM

Movers & Shakers – Volume 1 | Peter J Snow OAM

First published in 2026 by BeInspiredBooks.com
on behalf of Peter J Snow OAM

© Peter J Snow OAM 2026
The moral rights of the author have been asserted

All rights reserved. Except as permitted under the *Australian CopyrightAct1968*

(for example, a fair dealing for the purposes of study, research, criticism or review), no part of this book may be reproduced, stored in a retrieval system, communicated or transmitted in any form or by any means without prior written permission.

All inquiries should be made to the author.

Creator: Snow, Peter, author.

Title: Not Ordinary Lives 2, Movers & Shakers – Vol. 1 / Peter J Snow OAM.

ISBN: 978-1-923358-70-6 (Paperback)

ISBN: 978-1-923358-99-7 (PDF version)

ISBN: 978-1-923358-98-0 (ePub)

ISBN: 978-1-923358-97-3 (Audiobook)

Subjects: Ordinary people doing Extraordinary things.
Aspirational, Inspirational and Motivational.

A catalogue record for this book is available from the National Library of Australia

Paperback Printed by: IngramSpark
Publisher: BeInspiredBooks.com
Project management: Community & Corporate Marketing and Public Relations
Cover design by Synergy Graphics
Cover photo by Ian Ritchie

Disclaimer

The material in this publication is of the nature of general comment only and does not represent professional advice. It is not intended to provide specific guidance for particular circumstances and it should not be relied on as the basis for any decision to take action or not take action on any matter which it covers. Readers should obtain professional advice where appropriate, before making any such decision.

To the maximum extent permitted by law, the author and publisher disclaim all responsibility and liability to any person, arising directly or indirectly from any person taking or not taking action based on the information in this publication.

Foreword

This is not a book of full biographies—and that is by design.

Not Ordinary Lives – Movers & Shakers, Volume 1 presents a series of short, semi-biographical portraits of people who have made a meaningful and lasting impact. Each story is a focused snapshot, capturing the moments, values, and decisions that shaped an extraordinary life.

Designed to be read in five to ten minutes, these memoirs are concise, engaging, and intentionally accessible—offering inspiration without excess.

Many of the stories are introduced through the author's personal connection with the subject, adding authenticity and depth.

These are not distant profiles, but reflections informed by firsthand experience and long-standing respect.

Unlike *The Tribe* series, which is united by a shared connection to a football club, the *Movers & Shakers* collection is linked by achievement and influence.

The individuals featured here have excelled across business, leadership, entrepreneurship, and community service.

Some reinvented themselves entirely; others built significant careers while maintaining a strong commitment to giving back.

For many, that commitment was shaped through involvement with JCI and its philosophy of personal development through community involvement.

The author has been uniquely placed to observe these journeys and has selected these stories as examples of lives lived with purpose.

They are included not for titles or accolades alone, but because their resilience, leadership, and service continue to inspire.

Not Ordinary Lives – Movers & Shakers, Volume 1 is the third collection in the ***Not Ordinary Lives*** series—a celebration of ambition, contribution, and the power of individuals who choose to make a difference.

Dedication

This book is dedicated to three truly extraordinary Movers & Shakers who passed away within months of one another in late 2025.

Though drawn from diverse backgrounds and professions, they were united through their membership of Jaycees (now known as JCI), the world's leading personal development organisation for people under 40 years of age.

Their shared commitment to leadership, service, and community left a lasting imprint on all who knew them.

The author was privileged to serve alongside each of them on the Board of The Jaycees Community Foundation Inc. for more than 35 years, witnessing first-hand their unwavering dedication to community service. Central to that legacy was the Foundation's flagship project—Albany's Historic Whaling Station at Discovery Bay, Albany in Western Australia. It is an enduring example of how vision, volunteer leadership, and collective effort can transform a derelict community asset into an internationally recognised cultural heritage landmark

This book is offered in gratitude and remembrance of three remarkable Movers & Shakers, great friends, and Life Members of a unique charity—whose commitment and legacy have made Australia a better place.

ABOVE: NEVILLE CLARE - GEOFF HAMPTON - RON RAYNOR
ALL JCI SENATORS & LIFE MEMBERS OF THE JAYCEES COMMUNITY FOUNDATION INC

Geoff and Ron were part of the decision-making team on the Board of the Jaycees Foundation Ltd that resulted in the establishment of the publisher of this book - **BeInspiredBooks.com** and its mini-book division – **5-minutereads.com** as a not-for-profit publishing platform for authors.

Movers & Shakers Volume 1 is also dedicated to the countless members of JCI who, through quiet service and shared purpose, have worked to make their communities—and the world—a better place.

Seven of them are featured in this book.

About the Author

Peter J Snow OAM is an entrepreneur, community leader, and chronicler of lives shaped by service, resilience, and purpose.

Often described—only half-jokingly—as a "jack of all trades and master of none," he has instead turned a wide range of interests into a legacy of enduring impact.

After stepping away from early pursuits in engineering and accounting, Peter found direction, confidence, and lifelong purpose through JCI (formerly Jaycees International), joining Fremantle Jaycees in 1970.

The leadership training, networks, and values he gained there became the foundation for more than seven decades of entrepreneurial activity and community involvement.

Throughout his life, Peter has initiated, led, or supported projects across public relations, fundraising, education, heritage preservation, and assistance for people with disabilities—many of which achieved national and international recognition.

His entrepreneurial ventures have spanned diverse industries, while his community service has consistently focused on collaboration, mentoring, and leaving organisations stronger than he found them.

His contributions have been recognised with numerous honours.

These include an Order of Australia Medal for service to the community, the Western Australian Heritage Award for Voluntary Individual Contribution, a Paul Harris Fellowship from Rotary International, the title of Honorary Tarheel of North Carolina, and selection as a Community Torchbearer for the Sydney 2000 Olympic Games.

He holds life membership of eight community and sporting organisations.

Within JCI, Peter has been named Outstanding National Officer, Outstanding JCI Senator of the World, and one of the organisation's Inspiring Jaycees of the World.

He is a life member of JCI Australia and its international parent body and was named among JCI's 110 Influential Members as part of its 110th anniversary celebrations in 2025.

Through the *Not Ordinary Lives* series, Peter brings together his passion for storytelling and his belief that extraordinary impact is often created not by fame or fortune, but by ordinary people who choose to lead, serve, and persist.

His writing reflects a lifelong conviction that setbacks can become turning points, and that the true measure of success lies in the lives enriched along the way.

Charities to Benefit from this Book

This book is different to most others. Publishing rights have been granted to the Jaycees Foundation Ltd, a charitable foundation and its not-for-profit publishing platform supporting new authors (focussing on youth). It is hoped to unveil stories to inspire and motivate readers to optimise their own lives and, in doing so, align with the foundation's objective of making Australia a better place.

Also, as part of arrangements with the author, the subjects of this book have nominated a charity to receive their share of royalties from its sale in all formats.

The charities to benefit from the sales of this book are:

Amber Community (Vic)
Australian Junior Chamber Foundation Inc.
BirdLife Australia
Breast Cancer Care (WA)
Cancer Council WA
Fly2Foundation
Free the Hounds Inc
Life Flight Australia (Darling Downs)
Mettle Women Inc.
MND Association (WA)
Red Nose Ltd (SIDS)
Royal Flying Doctor Service (Western Region)
Sea Rescue Tasmania Inc.

I thank all those who have willingly contributed their time and stories and for using them to support their chosen charity.

... Peter J Snow OAM

Contents

Foreword	3
Dedication	5
About the Author	7
- *Peter J Snow OAM*	
Charity Beneficiaries	9

MEMOIRS

Les Bail	12
- *Leaving a Permanent Legacy*	
Rochelle Borton	20
- *Building People, Building Possibility*	
Sciona Browne	28
- *Surviving Survivor and a Tsunami*	
Dr Chris Denz	40
- *Persistence in Practice*	
Ross Fitzgerald	50
- *Combining Business and Sport*	
Geoff Hampton	60
- *Service, Steadiness, and Substance*	
Fred Harrington OAM	70
- *Steady Hands, Quiet Strength*	

MEMOIRS (continued)

Irene Harrington OAM   80
- *Making Waves and a Better World*

Kevin Judge   92
- *A Life of Integrity and Service*

Seva Mozhaev   104
- *From Tokmok to TikTok*

Carmelo Musca   114
- *From Weddings to Film-Maker*

Alan Nelson   126
- *Setting Personal Challenges*

Mette Nielsen   136
- *The Nordic Cracker Queen*
  - Life is for Living

Peter Reitano   148
- *A Life of Service and Commitment*

Bev Smith   156
- *Just Do It ... and Enjoy the Journey*

Karen Smythe   166
- *Choosing Positivity, Purpose and the Next Mission*

More by the Author   178

Les Bail

Leaving a Permanent Legacy

As is a common theme throughout the various memoirs, fate played a hand in an extraordinary way.

One April day in 1996, the 7.45 am ABC radio news announced the death of a well-known Albany businessman along with three others in an aircraft accident. The plane had crashed at Mt. Manypeaks, 35 km from Western Australia's oldest coastal town.

I mentally discounted the possibility of it being John Bell, who along with wife Jill, managed Australia's last whaling station in a form of partnership with The Jaycees Community Foundation Inc. As the Foundation's Director responsible for the project the prospect of it being our partner was unlikely. John had a plane charter business separate to our management arrangements. He and Jill had operated a small whaling museum in a Nissan hut just outside the whaling station until 1980. Our partnership was a logical business arrangement that had endured for 16 years since our Foundation had been gifted the derelict site in December 1980.

A few minutes later, that unpleasant thought became a shocking reality when John's daughter rang to confirm that it was indeed John who had died. Also killed in the crash was a state policeman, a customs officer and federal policeman. John's plane had been chartered for a drug surveillance run along the south coast when it stalled and pancaked into the 565m mountain.

With more than 13,000 flying hours, John was no novice and was known to be meticulous in his flight preparation and flying procedures. The reason for the crash remained a mystery until it was discovered that there had been a number of instances with that model of aircraft. When flying at a particular speed and angle, it had a propensity to stall. Given the likelihood of a reduction in height and speed to conduct the surveillance operation, this was the Coronial conclusion.

With no succession plan in place, the Foundation Board based 400 km away in Perth, faced a dilemma. How or who would take over the hands-on role of running a struggling tourist attraction based on what remained of Australia's last derelict whaling station?

After making the trip to Albany for John's funeral, I was confronted by the expected very large crowd. Fortunately, one I had previously met through John was local Gary Tonkin. Gary is regarded as the world's greatest living scrimshander (an engraver of ivory like whale teeth - an ancient art of whalers going back to the early days of whaling). He had been close to John having regularly bought whale teeth that John had accumulated over the years as the whale spotting pilot for the now defunct whaling company. Gary introduced me to a larger than life and genial fellow – one Les Bail – a local dive boat and whale watch operator who also ran a salvage yard.

Les was a registered builder with a heritage leaning – a unique combination that perfectly fitted the role to be filled. Gary indicated that Les might be able to help us out for three months or so, while we found a replacement manager for the late John Bell.

That was to commence an enduring friendship with Les and his very supportive wife Dorothy and a business relationship that lasted not just three months - but more than 13 years. It also saw the creation of the run-down industrial complex into the iconic award-winning heritage tourist attraction that is known today as Discovery Bay.

After retiring following ten years as its General Manager, Les stayed on to project manage the development of the Foundation's Albany Biodiversity Park on the adjoining degraded bushland. This now boasts an Australian wildlife park, a regional flora exhibit featuring a living floral mural, wetlands and water recycling exhibits and a grassed amphitheatre that can seat 2,000.

Ironically, Les had had an earlier involvement with the whaling station. As President of South Coast Diving Club, in consultation with John Bell, he had overseen the scuttling of the whaling station's most decrepit whalechaser, the Cheynes III. This was after it had been stripped of all useful components and was destined for a second life as a diving practice wreck. Les's dive charter business had another site for learners to explore.

So who is Les Bail?

Leslie John Bail, affectionately known as Les, emerged into the world in February 1944, in the picturesque town of Albany, nestled along the rugged coastline of Western Australia. Born to Victor and Lorraine Bail, Les was the eldest of four siblings, growing up alongside his brothers Frederick, Wayne, and Kim. From the outset, it was evident that Les possessed a restless spirit and an insatiable curiosity about the world around him.

Raised in a household where hard work and integrity were esteemed above all else, Les learned the value of perseverance and determination from his parents. Despite not being academically inclined, he exhibited a natural aptitude for hands-on work, often spending his days tinkering in the family garage or exploring the great outdoors with his brothers.

After completing his education at Albany Senior High School, Les wasted no time in pursuing his passion for carpentry and joinery. At the tender age of 15, he embarked on a five-year apprenticeship, eagerly soaking up the knowledge and skills imparted by seasoned craftsmen. Under their guidance, Les honed his abilities, mastering the art of woodworking with precision and finesse.

Upon completing his apprenticeship, Les ventured into contracting, partnering with a colleague to establish Reader and Bail Building Contractors.

After 10 years Dorothy and Les purchased Terry Reader's share and commenced Jelda Holdings trading as LJ & DE Bail Building Contractors. Together, they tackled a myriad of projects, from residential renovations to commercial construction, earning a reputation for their exceptional craftsmanship and attention to detail.

As the years passed, Les's entrepreneurial spirit continued to drive him forward.

In 1977, he seized upon a new opportunity, founding Drive-in Timber & Salvage, a bustling business that catered to the needs of builders and DIY enthusiasts alike. Named because of its location conveniently opposite the local drive-in theatre, the salvage yard quickly became a hub of activity, offering a treasure trove of reclaimed materials and second-hand goods.

In addition to his burgeoning carpentry career, Les harboured a deep passion for diving and underwater exploration.

In 1978, recognizing a need for professional dive services in the community, He founded Southcoast Diving Supplies, providing equipment and expertise to recreational and commercial divers alike.

The dive shop quickly became a hub for enthusiasts, fostering a vibrant diving community within Albany.

Although hockey was his chosen sport at high school that he continued for some time when working, Les enjoyed Friday night tennis at Emu Point until his apprenticeship was completed.

Small bore rifle shooting was an enjoyable pastime with his father until work intervened. Scuba diving and photography were to become a later passion.

The acquisition of a 100-acre property on the edge of Wilson Inlet near Denmark on Western Australia's south coast provided weekends of relaxation, hunting and fishing.

Throughout his life, Les remained deeply committed to his community, volunteering his time and expertise to a variety of organizations and causes. With his marriage to Dorothy approaching six decades, he has had the support of a loving partner in all his endeavours and they have shared many adventures together.

Through his service as President of the Albany Photographic Society and the Western Australian Photographic Foundation, Chairman of the Albany Visitor Centre and President of Albany branch of SKAL International, Les has left an indelible mark on his community. And that doesn't include his roles on the Boards of the Albany Boat Shed, Great Southern Regional Tourism, Albany Tourist Bureau, Main Street Committee and various other specialist community projects.

Although Les has been recognised with Life Memberships of Albany Maritime Heritage Association Inc, Albany Photographic Society, The Jaycees Community Foundation Inc, a Centenary Medal and was a finalist in the 2007 Western Australian Heritage Awards, he has left a more permanent legacy.

His most fulfilling role was overseeing the development of the Discovery Bay Tourism Precinct based on built and natural heritage, and this is a permanent gift to the region he called home for most of his life.

Despite facing numerous challenges along the way, including financial setbacks and personal loss, Les approached each obstacle with courage and determination. His unwavering commitment to honesty and integrity served as a guiding light, inspiring those around him to strive for excellence in all they did.

As Les reflects on his life's journey, he does so with a profound sense of gratitude for the opportunities he's been given and the relationships he's formed along the way. His story serves as a testament to the power of hard work, perseverance, and the unwavering belief in oneself to overcome any obstacle that stands in the way of achieving one's dreams.

Les Bail's legacy lives on in the hearts and minds of all who have had the privilege of knowing him, a true pioneer and pillar of his community.

Rochelle Borton

Building People, Building Possibility

In my four years as Chairman of the Australian JCI Senate Group, it was always a privilege to present the international organisation's highest honour—a JCI Senatorship, which confers life membership of JCI. These presentations, usually made at the JCI Australia National Convention, were more than ceremonial. They marked moments when the organisation formally acknowledged individuals whose service and leadership had left a lasting imprint.

The COVID-19 pandemic, however, disrupted more than travel plans. In 2020 it reduced the National Convention to a series of small, state-based hubs in Brisbane, Wollongong and Melbourne, and in doing so denied me the opportunity to personally present a JCI Senatorship to one such outstanding mover and shaker—Rochelle Borton.

As I read through the breadth of achievements that supported her nomination, I found myself wondering how it was possible to accomplish so much while also being the mother of six children and running a business.

That question quickly turned into admiration, and then into confidence, when I learned that Rochelle was keen to take an active role on the Australian Junior Chamber Foundation Board.

With that knowledge, my decision to withdraw my own nomination for a second term—thereby avoiding the need for an election—was an easy one.

Rochelle's subsequent succession of Mark Horrocks as Chair of the Foundation has only confirmed the wisdom of that decision.

For those unfamiliar with how such leadership, resilience and capacity came to be, Rochelle's story provides the answer.

There is a particular kind of confidence that doesn't announce itself loudly but is impossible to ignore. It shows up in the way someone asks better questions, steps forward when others hesitate, and keeps moving even when the path is uncertain. Rochelle Borton has carried that confidence since childhood—not as bravado, but as an instinctive belief that growth is both possible and necessary.

Born in Camden, New South Wales, in July 1979, Rochelle grew up as one of four children in a family where curiosity was encouraged and horizons were deliberately widened. Her parents, Paul and Phyllis Everill, believed that learning did not stop at the classroom door, and that exposure to the world was itself an education.

That philosophy would shape Rochelle profoundly.

Her early years were marked by movement—both physical and intellectual. At twelve, the family relocated to Port Lincoln in South Australia, and later, when Rochelle was sixteen, to San Francisco in the United States.

These were not simply changes of address; they were formative experiences that taught her adaptability, perspective and courage. Living abroad as a teenager expanded her sense of what was possible and planted a lasting appreciation for diversity, exploration and reinvention.

School, for Rochelle, was a place of connection rather than confinement. She was outspoken, curious and unembarrassed about stepping up or standing out. Teachers and adults found her easy to engage; peers often followed her lead. She loved learning, not just for achievement, but for what it unlocked in people. Even an early disappointment—being quietly edged out of a friendship group—left a lasting imprint. It wasn't rejection that troubled her most, but the ease with which loyalty could be influenced. From that moment, she vowed never to diminish others to belong herself.

Sport played its own role in shaping Rochelle's resilience.

As a competitive netballer, water polo player and swimmer, she learned discipline, teamwork and how to push through discomfort—skills that would later reappear in boardrooms, classrooms and community leadership roles. Winning mattered, but so did effort, preparation and self-respect.

Her professional journey began in roles that placed her close to decision-makers and complex systems.

As an Executive Assistant across major organisations—including Westpac Bank, Bankers Trust, BHP (later BlueScope Steel) and the University of Wollongong—Rochelle developed a deep understanding of how institutions function, and where they often fail the people within them. She was rarely content to simply manage tasks; she wanted to understand purpose, process and impact.

That curiosity propelled her into project leadership roles at both the University of Wollongong and the University of Sydney, and later into executive leadership within the Leadership Illawarra Program at Sydney Business School. Alongside formal qualifications—a Master of Business Administration in Management, a Graduate Diploma in Psychology, and certifications in ProPlay and LEGO® Serious Play®—she was refining a distinctive approach: build people first, and systems will follow.

It was during these years that Rochelle's philosophy began to crystallise. Growth, she believed, was not optional. If a better way could be seen, there was an obligation to move toward it—and to help others do the same. Strengths should be amplified before deficits dissected. Agency mattered. Meaning mattered more than appearances.

In 2016, Rochelle took a decisive step, founding Eduinfluencers. Entrepreneurship was exhilarating—but unforgiving. The early years demanded hustle, consistency and an unwavering belief that the work mattered, even when the outcomes were uncertain. There were moments of doubt, financial strain and personal exhaustion. Still, she kept showing up, driven by a personal mantra: be one per cent better every single day.

Nearly a decade later, that persistence culminated not only in a thriving business, but in the confidence to open a second venture—SENSE Training Australia—in 2025. It was not a pivot away from her purpose, but a deeper commitment to it.

Parallel to her professional life ran an extraordinary commitment to service through JCI (formerly Junior Chamber International). What began as involvement at a local level grew into a defining feature of Rochelle's leadership identity. Over more than twenty years, JCI became what she half-jokingly refers to as her most demanding "hobby"—one that required time, money, emotional investment and, occasionally, blood, sweat and tears. Her leadership trajectory through JCI was both national and global: local director roles in Illawarra and Sydney, National President of JCI Australia in 2016, International Vice President in 2018, and ongoing service as a global training mentor.

Along the way, she travelled to more than thirty countries, delivered countless leadership programs and mentored hundreds of emerging leaders. She did not simply hold titles; she built capability, confidence and courage in others.

Recognition followed—not as a goal, but as a by-product. Awards across education, business and community service acknowledged her influence, including multiple teaching excellence awards, national business accolades, international recognition through JCI, and service honours from Lions Clubs. Yet those who know Rochelle well understand that her proudest success is not listed on any certificate.

That success is family. Rochelle is the mother of six children—four biological and two stepchildren—each of whom she speaks about with fierce pride. Motherhood reshaped her sense of identity and purpose, beginning with the birth of her first daughter in 2004. Later, the breakdown of her marriage forced another period of reckoning—one that challenged her assumptions about self, stability and strength. It was painful, disorienting and deeply personal. But it also reinforced her belief that it is never too late to change direction, rewrite expectations, or choose growth over fear.

Throughout every season, Rochelle has drawn inspiration from mentors—none more enduring than her father. His coaching approach, his refusal to prescribe answers, and his ability to guide her toward her own decisions left a lasting imprint. Other female leaders early in her career modelled a form of leadership that was both exacting and affirming, supporting her strengths while addressing shortcomings with care.

Rochelle strives to lead the same way, acknowledging that she doesn't always get it right—but always learns.

Adversity, when it appears, is met head-on. Rochelle's instinct is to engage, to solve, to push through. She competes with herself as much as anyone else, and expects others to claim agency over their own growth. It doesn't always land comfortably, but it builds resilience, pride and momentum.

Relaxation, for Rochelle, is less about stillness than renewal. She finds joy in her work, sanctuary in audiobooks and podcasts, and restoration in deliberate pauses—lying beside a beach or pool, devices switched off, marvelling at the scale of the world and her place within it.

Asked what matters most, her answer is both simple and demanding: live a full life. Stay away from unnecessary drama. Keep a small circle built on love and mutual hope. Choose purpose over comfort. Amaze others—not through performance, but through integrity. Leave people and places better than you found them.

And above all, remember this: change is always possible. No matter the age, the chapter, or the circumstances—it is never, ever too late.

Sciona Browne

Surviving Survivor and a Tsunami

As so often happens, it was not planning but circumstance that first brought Sciona Browne into my life.

At the time, Bruce Gallash and I were growing an increasingly complex venture capital business. What had begun as an entrepreneurial exercise had reached the point where governance, structure and execution demanded more than enthusiasm and long hours. We needed an executive director—someone who could see *what might be*, who understood precision and risk, and who possessed an instinct for opportunity without losing sight of detail.

Sciona stood out almost immediately.

Her résumé alone suggested an uncommon mind: Australia's first woman test pilot, with a career forged in environments where accuracy is non-negotiable and error unforgiving. Attention to detail, in her case, was not a learned discipline—it was intrinsic. She joined the Evandale House Group team and it did not take long for her influence to be felt. She brought clarity, calm judgement, and a way of seeing beyond the immediate horizon.

It was those same qualities that prompted me to see her as an ideal fit for another role altogether. At the time, I was chairing The Jaycees Community Foundation. My commercial commitments were increasingly limiting the time I could devote to the Foundation.

The need for steady, capable leadership was becoming apparent. Sciona accepted a part-time CEO role, and as things progressed it became clear that the Foundation's flagship project—the future development of Albany's Historic Whaling Station—could no longer be managed on a part-time basis.

Around that same period, a significant health scare forced me to reassess my own priorities. Quietly, perceptively, and without fanfare, Sciona approached one of the elder statesmen on the Foundation's Board. Rather than looking outward for a full-time CEO, she suggested they consider a different option: that I transition from a non-executive chairmanship to a full-time Executive Chairman role, allowing continuity, commitment and passion for the project to align.

The Board agreed.

Timing, as I have written elsewhere, is everything. That decision saw me wind down my commercial interests, accept a pay cut, and relocate with my wife to a small cottage on Albany's whaling station—three intense, demanding and ultimately rewarding years that produced an award-winning outcome of which our entire team remains justifiably proud.

For that remarkable chapter of my life, I have Sciona Browne to thank. But that is only a small part of her story.

To understand Sciona properly—to appreciate the depth of her resilience, curiosity and quiet courage—you need to know where she came from, the spaces she has crossed, and the challenges she has never shied away from.

Because Sciona Browne has never been afraid of open space.

Not the vast red horizons of the Northern Territory where she ran barefoot as a child. Not the cold, rolling swell of the Southern Ocean where survival meant grit, teamwork, and will. Not the empty sky where a single-seat aircraft tests both design and courage. And not the quiet inner terrain where the hardest questions of meaning and purpose are asked.

She was born on 13 April 1952 in Canberra, the eldest of five children to Jess and Claude Browne. Her father was a Royal Australian Air Force pilot, which meant that stability was a luxury the family never quite owned. Nine schools in five years. New accents, new uniforms, new expectations. Every state with its own curriculum. Every move another reset.

"I hated school," she says plainly, without bitterness—just truth. But outside the classroom, life was expansive. Especially in the Northern Territory. There, childhood was not fenced in by schedules or bells. It was bushland and dust and freedom. It was long days roaming country that felt infinite, learning to read land and weather instinctively. It was, eventually, a dog.

Her first dog—a blue heeler mix known as a Lake Nash Heeler—was bred near an RAAF base in the Territory. That dog became her anchor. In a childhood defined by transience, the dog stayed. It was her companion, her confidant, her first lesson in loyalty.

Years later, she would say that everything important she learned early came not from schoolrooms, but from bush tracks, animals, and silence.

Initially, her adult ambitions followed a different trajectory. She enrolled at Murdoch University to study veterinary science. Animals made sense. Systems, however, did not. University life failed to ignite her, and she left before completing the degree. What followed might have looked like indecision to some—but for Sciona, it was simply listening for the right current.

That current arrived in the form of aviation—and a man named Alec MacDonald. Alec was a retired Air Force pilot, a quietly formidable figure with deep technical skill and a generosity of spirit that would change the course of her life. Through mutual friends, Sciona met Alec and his business partner, Sue Folks, as they were forming Rottnest Airlines—running charter flights between Perth and Rottnest Island.

At first, Sciona worked as what she jokingly calls an "office gopher." Filing. Organising. Helping wherever needed. But she was watching. Listening. Absorbing.

Alec noticed. "*He took me under his wing,*" she says. Literally.

Flying wasn't entirely foreign—her own father had been a pilot—but he had discouraged her from aviation. In that era, women pilots were rare and often unwelcome. Jobs were scarce. The risks were high. The pathways unclear.

But Alec saw capability where others saw limitation.

He was building aircraft himself—home-built designs based on Burt Rutan's Long-EZ, a distinctive tandem two-seater with a canard wing. Sciona helped him build it. Carbon fibre. Electrics. Mechanics. She learned from the inside out.

Flying stopped being an abstract dream. It became practical, technical, embodied. From there, aviation took her further than she could ever have predicted.

The Graham family were developing a radical aircraft design—spin-proof, lightweight, made of composite materials, intended for vast cattle stations where four-wheel drives were slow and inefficient. They formed Eagle Aircraft. Experts were brought from the United States. Alec was enlisted for his experience. Sciona followed, again learning, again observing.

When government funding collapsed after a change of administration, the project nearly died. But eventually, investment came from Malaysia's Petronas.

The program resumed—larger, more ambitious.

Flight testing followed. Certification. Precision. Risk.

Sciona was working on the factory floor when the testing phase moved to Cunderdin, a disused Air Force strip. The team included engineers, designers, and Harry Bradford—the former Chief Test Pilot of the Royal Australian Air Force.

She was the only woman. She didn't ask for special treatment. She asked for responsibility.

She was invited onto the flight test team. Not as chief test pilot—that role remained with Harry—but as part of the core group. When production began, every aircraft rolling off the line had to be tested individually.

Sciona became that pilot.

In doing so, she became the first female test pilot in the Southern Hemisphere.

She does not dramatise this achievement. She states it the way pilots state facts: cleanly, without embellishment. Yet it stands as one of the quiet milestones of Australian aviation.

Recognition followed. The Nancy-Bird Walton Award from the Australian Women Pilots' Association—honouring the most noteworthy contribution to aviation by a woman in Australasia. It mattered. But titles were never her motivation.

What drove Sciona was challenge.

Which is why, years later, when her mother asked her to record the final episode of the American television show *Survivor*, she watched it—and felt something spark.

When the casting call for the first Australian *Survivor* aired, she applied.

Why not? she thought.

Exotic locations. A $500,000 prize. Sixteen contestants.

A test of endurance, bush skills, resilience. She had all three.

Out of 8,500 applicants, she made the final sixteen.

What followed was secrecy, aliases, non-disclosure agreements, weeks confined to a North Sydney hotel room with meals left outside the door. Psychological testing. Interrogative screen tests designed to provoke emotional fracture.

"We're out there together and I hate your guts," one producer barked. *"How do you handle that?"*

Sciona stayed calm. At home in Perth, she trained relentlessly.

Jacob's Ladder at Kings Park—242 concrete steps overlooking the Swan River—sometimes twice a day.

Gym sessions. Weight gain. Mental preparation.

She worried less about the physical challenges than the social ones. *"I'm not very gregarious,"* she admits. *"I like my own space."*

So she saw a sports psychologist. Not to harden herself—but to understand herself.

When filming began at Whaler's Way, South Australia, it was nothing like modern *Survivor*. No lavish rewards. No wine and cake. Rations equivalent to prisoners of war. A bag of white rice. That was it.

The winter in the Great Australian Bight was one of the coldest in a decade. During one challenge, she and fellow contestant Katie developed hypothermia so severe that medics debated hospitalisation. They were wrapped together in sleeping bags, shivering, teeth chattering uncontrollably.

"I knew I would win that challenge," Sciona says quietly. Years of windsurfing had taught her how to read water, manage cold, and hold ground.

She did. And she endured.

From the moment she boarded the bus in Adelaide, Sciona was assessing. Who to trust. Who to avoid. At the back of the bus, she watched every contestant arrive.

One stood out—Rob Dickson. Former AFL player. Helicopter pilot. Fit. Strategic.

They formed an alliance on day one and held it through the game.

Sciona finished runner-up. Rob won.

Later, Rob and his two sons would die in a car accident in South Africa. His wife Dusty survived.

Sciona does not dwell on this tragedy—but it sits with her, as loss often does. Quietly. Permanently.

After *Survivor*, adventure did not loosen its grip. She sailed around the world on a 60-foot steel yacht—but only on one condition: she would learn to sail properly.

Then came Christmas Day, 2004. Phi Phi Don Island.

She was preparing to scuba dive when the sea withdrew—as though a plug had been pulled from the bay.

Instinct took over. The tsunami came.

They survived by heading into deep water, the yacht's bow angled into the surge. The destruction was absolute. Boats overturned. Villages erased. Bodies later lined the shore in black bags.

For weeks, they assisted with recovery efforts. Relayed emergency communications. Helped hospitals.

It was, she says simply, *"terrible."*

Back in Australia, another chapter unfolded—one less visible, but no less meaningful.

For forty years, Sciona has been involved with the Integral Yoga Association of Western Australia. In her early twenties, she lived in an ashram in Fremantle. Not as an escape—but as inquiry.

Yoga, for her, was never religion. It was a way of asking better questions.

A Swami once told her, *"You will never be satisfied with someone else's answer. Ask the questioner the question!"*

She has lived that advice ever since.

In the Kimberley, she worked with Aboriginal communities—helping establish programs for young women, advocating education, opening pathways where few existed.

She cycles. Long distances. Hundreds of kilometres a week. Competitive cycling came late—but at an age when many slow down, she accelerated. Even in her seventies, she holds her own against riders decades younger.

Asked how she handles adversity, her answer is unwavering.

"Stay focused. Never give up."

If there is one lesson Sciona Browne offers, it is this: limits are often beliefs masquerading as facts.

She has crossed oceans, outlasted storms, flown experimental aircraft, survived disaster, and endured cold, hunger, and loss—not by bravado, but by persistence.

She has never waited for permission.

And she has never stopped moving forward—eyes on the horizon, feet on the ground, mind open, unafraid of the vastness ahead.

Because for Sciona Browne, an ordinary life was never an option.

Dr Chris Denz

Persistence in Practice

Some people make noise when they move through the world. Others make foundations.

Dr Chris Denz belongs firmly to the latter group.

My introduction to Chris was, like many of the most consequential encounters in life, indirect and entirely unplanned. It came through my late mentor Bill Ross, a man whose quiet wisdom shaped many careers—including, as it turned out, both Chris's and mine.

Bill had retained me to assess the commercial potential of a bespoke medical practice management software system developed by the major partner of a medical centre he chaired. It was clever software, ahead of its time, but the market was brutally concentrated. Two dominant players controlled more than 90 per cent of the field, and doctors—understandably risk-averse—would be reluctant to experiment with a virtually unknown system.

After careful research, I concluded that any attempt to commercialise the software would require substantial funding and a lengthy *"try before you buy"* model simply to gain a foothold. In good conscience, I could not recommend spending serious money on a venture I believed would likely fail. Instead, I suggested licensing its unique features to one of the major providers and declined to submit an account for my time.

That honesty struck a chord.

A year or so later, Bill—then in his early eighties and after seventeen years as independent chairman of one of Perth's busiest medical centres—decided it was time to step back. A great believer in succession planning, he asked whether I would consider taking over his role and, with my consent, put my name forward to his board. It was supported by a summary of my business experience in lieu of a formal CV which, after 30 years of self-employment, I had previously had no need of.

That was how I came to meet Chris Denz for the second time—as founder, senior partner and managing director of the medical centre Bill had chaired for nearly two decades. The interview was refreshingly brief. After speaking to my hastily produced business profile, I asked whether there were any questions.

The reply was simple: *"No—if Bill reckons you're okay, you're okay with us."*

Over the decade that followed, attempting to fill Bill's shoes, I had the privilege of working alongside Chris and seeing firsthand the depth of his commitment—to staff, to patients, and to doing things properly even when no one was watching.

It is a story of business and personal success.

Christopher Robin Denz was born on 21 July 1959 in Huntly, New Zealand, the second of four children to John (Austine Herbert) and Lenore Denz. His early years were shaped by family, movement, and the outdoors.

Childhood meant cubby houses constructed both inside the family home and out in the yard, long beach holidays, and trout fishing trips with his father in the lakes—moments of connection and freedom that left a lasting imprint.

School life, however, was not always gentle. Chris describes himself as gawky, cheeky, nerdy, skinny and smart—a combination that can draw attention for the wrong reasons. He was bullied at both primary and high school. Although never physically assaulted, the fear was real and persistent. His saving grace was speed. Chris was a fast runner—exceptionally fast—and when chased, he usually escaped.

There is something quietly symbolic in that image: a boy learning early that survival often comes down to endurance, pace, and refusing to stop.

Despite those experiences, Chris enjoyed school and remembers it fondly.

A scholarship to boarding school at Sacred Heart College in Glen Innes became a pivotal moment. The structure, discipline and opportunity it provided altered the course of his life, opening the door to university and, eventually, medical school.

It reinforced a belief that would guide him throughout his life—that hard work, personal accountability and persistence are non-negotiable.

In 1978, Chris entered Otago University to study medicine. The journey was demanding in every sense. Financially, there was no safety net. To support himself, he worked wherever work could be found—brick making, road construction, a tannery, a dairy factory producing butter, and a warehouse job sorting car parts for British Motor Corporation.

None of it glamorous. All of it necessary.

When he graduated in December 1983, Chris regarded his medical degree not as a badge of status, but as a passport—a means to contribute, to build, and to serve. It remains, in his own words, the most important "award" of his life because it set everything else in motion.

After completing an elective in Vancouver, Canada, and his intern year in Tauranga, New Zealand, Chris faced a professional impasse. Unable to secure his preferred position in his home country, he made the decision to move to Australia. It was not a dramatic leap of faith—just a practical response to circumstance.

He worked first in Tasmania, in private emergency medicine at St Helens Hospital, before arriving in Western Australia in 1986.

Opportunity, as it turned out, often arrives wearing the clothes of disappointment.

By then, Chris had worked in enough medical practices to know that many things could be done better. Systems were inefficient, facilities poorly designed, and administration too often interfered with patient care. He wanted to practise medicine without feeling as though he was constantly "walking uphill in the snow."

So he decided to build something different.

In 1986, Chris purchased a general practice in West Perth. At the same time, recognising that clinical excellence alone would not sustain a growing enterprise, he undertook postgraduate business studies at Curtin University.

On 6 February 1989, Forrest Chase Medical Centre opened its doors. It was the result of vision, risk, and relentless effort.

The early years were gruelling. Chris worked extraordinary hours—twelve-hour days, thirty days in a row, many times over—doing whatever was required to keep the practice viable.

His philosophy was clear and uncompromising: quality before quantity; equal pay for equal work; reward effort; don't do unprofitable work; and never confuse activity with progress.

"You never go broke making a profit," he would often say, not as a slogan, but as a statement of reality.

Challenges arrived regularly and without warning. A Supreme Court lease challenge in 1996 threatened the very foundation of the business. Chris fought it and won. Later came the development of Central City Medical Centre atop Perth's Central Railway Station—five times the size of the original practice—bringing with it complexity, risk, and heightened responsibility.

Through every challenge, persistence was the constant.

Chris is the first to acknowledge that he did not do it alone. Central to his journey was Bill Ross, who took a young, energetic doctor with plenty of ideas but little business experience under his wing. For nearly twenty years, Bill provided guidance, perspective and restraint—often preventing enthusiasm from becoming overreach. Chris credits Bill with shaping not just his professional success, but key parts of his character.

In late 2013, at the age of fifty-five, Chris received a diagnosis that would test everything he believed about resilience.

Throat cancer. For most people, such news is frightening. For a doctor, fully aware of the statistics and potential outcomes, it carries an added psychological weight. Chris's first concern was not himself, but his family.

The diagnosis came on a Friday—the same day his son Zac finished medical school in Queensland and was about to sit major exams. Chris's wife Chin was over there with him. After discussion, they decided to tell both their children immediately rather than delay.

Chris made one request of his son: "*Focus on your exams. Do well. The last thing I want to worry about during treatment is whether you need to re-sit supplementary exams.*"

Then Chris went to work—not in the clinic, but in the literature. He immersed himself in medical journals, uncovering emerging research showing that HPV-16 related throat cancers, when optimally treated, had cure rates exceeding ninety per cent. Armed with information, he sought multiple specialist opinions, looking for consistency rather than heroics.

When professional boundaries blurred—as they often do when a doctor becomes a patient—Chin stepped in decisively, reminding one specialist that Chris was the patient, not the doctor, and that she would ensure he did exactly what a good patient should do.

On medical advice, Chris stopped working immediately to minimise any risk of infection from patients that could potentially disrupt treatment. The practice continued to operate smoothly, exactly as it had been designed to do.

Partners and staff stepped up without hesitation.

Chris focused on preparation—exercise, nutrition, discipline. At one point he became almost too fit, losing weight to the alarm of his radiotherapist who promptly ordered him to exercise less and eat more.

The treatment worked.

Some pleasures were lost—such as the enjoyment of a good red wine—but perspective was gained. In 2023, another health challenge followed: this time prostate cancer. Once again, Chris approached it methodically and responsibly. Surgery and follow-up treatment were successful, and he returned to full health and full engagement in the business.

Resilience, for Chris, is not loud. It is organised.

Beyond medicine, Chris has lived an active and engaged life. Athletics shaped his youth; he was a formidable mile runner. He played rugby through university, cricket and baseball at school, squash and tennis until a shoulder injury at fifty, and golf until cancer interrupted that chapter. He relaxes by reading—physics, autobiographies, business—and enjoys science fiction films.

Community service has always mattered. He joined the St George's Rotary Club in 1989, later becoming president, and spent over a decade contributing to community initiatives. He also served ten years on the board of WA Opera, stepping down only when health required it.

At the centre of everything has been family. Chris and Chin married in February 1989 and have built a life grounded in mutual respect, shared values and resilience. Together they raised their two children, Zachary and Jessica, and navigated challenges that would have fractured lesser partnerships. Chris counts that marriage among his greatest successes.

Ask Chris Denz what matters most, and the answers are simple. Justice. Accountability. Effort.

"It is what you do, not what you say that counts," he says. *"There is no free ride. If you want something, make it happen."*

The single most important lesson he offers is resilience. Never give up on your dreams. Hard work and persistence—in large enough doses—can overcome almost any challenge.

Chris Denz did not set out to be extraordinary.

He set out to do things properly. To build systems that worked. To treat people fairly. To persist when it would have been easier to stop.

In the end, that may be the most extraordinary legacy of all.

Ross Fitzgerald

Combining Business and Sport

Anyone who has followed the fortunes of Swan Districts for at least the last two decades knows that home games are played on an oval named after Australia's leading industrial boot. That can be attributed to the foresight of a 1982 premiership player and his mates who saw an opportunity to give back while simultaneously boosting their company's brand. What more appropriate pairing could one imagine than a football field and a boot. It was to be an enduring marriage consummated on hallowed turf with long term benefits to both partners.

Ross William Fitzgerald, better known to friends and colleagues as "Fitzy," is a name synonymous with resilience, ambition, and a genuine love for life. A no-nonsense, warm-hearted, and likable character, Fitzy's journey is a tale of hard-earned wisdom and remarkable achievements in both football and business.

With four work colleagues, he co-founded one of Australia's leading industrial footwear brands, Steel Blue.

Born in December 1959, to Colin and Phyllis Fitzgerald, Fitzy grew up in a modest environment, where ambition was often tempered by life's realities. School was never his strong suit; and with a limited concentration span, academics didn't hold his interest. However, sport – especially football and cricket – ignited a spark in him. Leaving Belmont Senior High School at 15, he knew one thing for certain: he wanted to play State League football.

His love for the game propelled him forward, making him a durable player in the world of Australian Rules football.

Fitzy's passion and dedication to sports led him to play league football for Swan Districts Football Club, racking up 112 games over seven seasons. Between 1978 and 1982, he left his mark as a forceful presence on the field, helping the team beat league leaders, Claremont, to clinch the club's first premiership in 20 years.

In that game, Swan Districts pulled off an incredible performance, with the team's unity and determination shining through. He would later look back on that game as one of the proudest moments of his career. The victory was especially sweet for Fitzy, as it validated years of hard work and sacrifice, not only for him but for his teammates, coaches, and the loyal Swan Districts fans who had supported the club through thick and thin.

The following season, circumstances saw him move to Perth Football Club, where he spent three seasons. While he continued to play at a high level, he found that he missed the camaraderie he had enjoyed at the home of the black and whites and returned to Swan Districts for his final two seasons. His 152-game league career ended in 1987 - still wearing guernsey No. 6 for all but one of his 112 games for Swan Districts.

Once his state league playing days were over, Fitzy captain-coached Brookton for two years.

This role allowed him to hone his leadership skills, working directly with younger, developing players in a club that didn't have access to the same resources and coaching staff as a State League club. His experiences as a player had taught him the value of discipline, teamwork, and community, and he was determined to pass these lessons on. His approach as a coach was demanding but fair; he believed in pushing players to reach their potential while fostering a supportive and inclusive team environment.

Fitzy's coaching journey eventually brought him back to the city, where he played at suburban club Maddington. Very dear to his heart is High Wycombe Amateur Football Club that he and a group of mates started and funded. He earned life membership having coached the club from 1992 to 2000 - apart from a two-year absence to become an assistant coach to Kevin Worthington at East Perth Football Club. Under his coaching, High Wycombe won its first premiership in 1995, with that year also marking the start of a remarkable business venture.

His coaching style combined the strategic acumen he had honed over years of playing with a deep respect for the game and its traditions. He emphasised the importance of mental toughness and resilience, values that guided him through both his sporting and business endeavours.

During the summer, he kept himself in trim playing his secondary sport of cricket, playing "A" grade for Perth for three seasons from 1976 and again in 1985/86.

From 1978 to 1993 he also played for Ascot Cricket Club (then known as Rivervale Cricket Club) of which he is a proud life member.

Fitzy's journey into business wasn't straightforward. During his sporting career, he ventured into various industries, trying to find his footing. He began with a carpentry apprenticeship but soon realised it wasn't his calling. He tried the transport industry, where he invested his $10,000 of savings into a small trucking business, only to face a heavy setback when the business failed, leaving him with significant losses. This tough experience was a turning point, teaching him the importance of caution in business and the resilience to keep pushing forward.

Determined, he switched to sales, briefly working as an account manager at a commercial radio station, then as manager of a sports store. He finally found some stability in shoe manufacturer, Comfortwear, where he gained valuable insights into the industry. Over time, Fitzy's roles expanded from purchasing to sales, eventually rising to be sales manager. But a shift in company ownership led to management changes that threatened to derail the business. he saw the writing on the wall, but rather than dwell on a failing situation, he decided to take a leap of faith that would change his life.

In 1995, Fitzy and four other work colleagues from his Comfortwear days put a Business Plan together to establish Steel Blue, a premium brand specialising in industrial footwear. The road to success was not smooth; within the first eight months, they lost half a million dollars – a figure five times their projected budget. However, his team remained undeterred. They identified a gap in the market for comfortable and safe industrial boots, recognising that traditional boots were basic lace-ups that often-neglected worker comfort and support.

They had initially named the company "Steel Dingo", and had all stationery printed when a cease-and-desist letter from solicitors representing an east coast business of the same name, forced a last-minute rebranding. "Steel Blue" became the hastily selected alternative. The team retained the original dingo head motif in their logo, and the new name soon became synonymous with quality and innovation in the industrial footwear market. Steel Blue's early years were challenging, but the team persevered, driven by their shared vision and camaraderie. They aimed to develop *"the world's most comfortable industrial boot,"* a promise that became the backbone of their brand's identity.

Over the next six years, Steel Blue struggled to break even, but the founders' resilience paid off. Their commitment to quality and comfort catapulted Steel Blue to the top of Australia's industrial footwear market, even earning them the prestigious Telstra Australian Small Business of the Year award. The boots became widely popular among Australian workers and beyond, setting new industry standards for safety and comfort. Steel Blue boots can now be found in more than 20 countries, ranking the company as one of Australia's great home-grown success stories.

Fitzy never forgot where he came from, nor did he lose sight of his connection to the community that had shaped him. Steel Blue became a major sponsor of Swan Districts Football Club, locking in naming rights for the club's home ground, now known as Steel Blue Oval, for more than 20 years.

His heart for giving extended beyond football, with the company allocating part of the sales of specific boots to two charities.

This has meant more than two and a half million dollars to Breast Cancer Care WA and Beyond Blue, two charities that aligned with the company's values and desire to make a meaningful impact.

Steel Blue's sponsorship efforts are part of a broader Board philosophy that Fitzy, as Chief Sales Officer of nearly 30 years, champions: *balance between commercial success and giving back*.

As he sees it, the real success lies not just in making profits but in uplifting communities, supporting local sport, and helping causes that matter.

As part of a branding strategy, the oval naming was leveraged by the appointment of recently retired sports stars such as cricket's legendary fast bowler DK Lillee and Queensland Broncos and State of Origin rugby league star Michael Hancock. Australian Rules stars were strategically selected by state - Glen Jakovich (W.A.); Mark Ricciuto (S.A.); and Glen Archer (Victoria). And it certainly worked.

For Fitzy, the journey from his early losses to co-founding a successful brand taught him invaluable lessons. Losing his savings in his first transport venture taught him resilience and the importance of thoughtful decision-making. Later, as Steel Blue evolved, he embraced a unique set of business principles that kept the company's spirit alive and thriving. Fitzy believes in a happy, people-oriented workplace where *"a hundred percent is made up of many one-percenters."* He values simplicity, constant improvement, and a *"team of huggers"* culture, where people feel valued and engaged.

As with most successful entrepreneurs, Fitzy has a friend and confidant, Peter Carter, with whom he has had great dialogue for over 50 years. Peter has been a successful businessman in his own right and a fellow part-owner of Steel Blue, upon whom he can rely.

His balance and calmness led to some sound decisions over the years for which Fitzy is most appreciative.

Outside of work, Fitzy and wife Kerryn, share a love for racing and pacing horses.

Originally dabbling in the sport of kings, their initial foray into pacing came when they bought a share in a New Zealand-bred horse named Rocknroll Lincoln for $13,000. To their surprise, the horse won several races and even clinched the 2019 WA Pacing Cup, bringing them a handsome $70,000 return.

This early success fuelled a deeper interest in both equine racing formats, and they have since enjoyed remarkable achievements in the field.

More than 200 wins, including 16 Group 1 races, is just reward for Fitzy's commitment to this form of relaxation away from business pressures.

His love for competition and excellence is reflected in this passion, showing that his drive extends well beyond the business realm.

His other escape is to spend time at home with Kerryn, watching sport on television, sharing a laugh and a glass or two of red wine of which he is an avid buyer. A visit to New York and Hawaii has prompted further plans to travel and more time with their two children and four grandsons.

Fitzy's story is one of a man who rose from humble beginnings, faced setbacks with grit, and help build a successful business with friends who shared his vision.

His journey reminds us that success isn't just about financial gain but about building something meaningful, giving back to the community, and living with purpose.

His approach to life – to enjoy every moment and work toward leaving the world a little better than he found it – is an inspiration to those around him.

Geoff Hampton
Service, Steadiness, and Substance

My first real connection with Geoff Hampton came in 1986, when he was appointed to the Board of The Jaycees Community Foundation Inc as Hamersley Jaycees' representative. It was a modest appointment on paper, but one that revealed, almost immediately, the calibre of the man. The Foundation itself was a unique charitable offshoot of the Western Australian branch of Australian Jaycees (now JCI Australia), and Geoff approached the role with the same quiet diligence and sense of responsibility that would define every commitment he undertook.

Over the next 39 years, through successive Board roles and shared service right up until his sudden passing in September 2025, that professional association deepened into a genuine friendship. What grew alongside it was a profound respect for a man whose contribution to community life was both extensive and understated. Geoff never sought recognition, yet it was impossible not to admire the consistency, integrity, and generosity with which he gave of himself—whether in governance, mentorship, or simple acts of support offered without expectation.

Some lives make headlines. Others build the scaffolding that holds communities together. Geoffrey William Hampton's life belonged firmly to the latter.

Born on 27 October 1949 in the Tasmanian town of Deloraine, Geoff lived a life defined not by noise or self-promotion, but by service, steady leadership, and an unshakeable commitment to family, profession, and community. He was not a man who sought centre stage. Instead, he preferred to work behind the scenes, ensuring that organisations functioned well, people were supported, and opportunities quietly opened for others.

Though his death came suddenly—barely a month after a diagnosis of liver cancer—it is clear to all who knew him that his life was already complete in its purpose. He had lived fully, generously, and with intention. He had loved deeply, served faithfully, and left institutions stronger than he found them.

In every meaningful sense, Geoff Hampton lived a life well.

Geoff was the son of George and Daphnie Hampton and grew up in a lively household alongside his siblings Valma, Kenneth, Judith, and later Pamela. Life in Deloraine was modest, grounded in hard work and mutual reliance. There was little excess, but there was no shortage of character-building experiences. From his parents, Geoff absorbed values that would remain constant throughout his life: honesty, reliability, humility, and an instinctive sense of responsibility to others.

At Deloraine High School, Geoff flourished. He enjoyed learning and the structure of school life, and he was naturally drawn to roles where he could contribute and help organise others.

Teachers recognised his maturity and calm demeanour, and in his final year he was appointed a Prefect—a moment of quiet pride that meant more to him for the trust it represented than for the title itself.

There were, however, early lessons in disappointment. As a keen young footballer, Geoff once missed out simply because his family could not afford football boots. It was a small incident in the scheme of life, but it left a lasting impression. Rather than breeding resentment, it instilled in him a quiet resolve: circumstances might limit resources, but they would never define character. Years later, that same resolve would underpin his generosity toward junior sport and youth development.

In 1967, shortly after leaving school, Geoff stepped into the professional world of insurance in Launceston. He began at the bottom, learning the industry patiently and thoroughly. Colleagues quickly came to trust his judgement and work ethic. Within three years he had progressed to Fire Clerk and then Inspector, roles that brought greater responsibility and independence. The company car that came with the Inspector's role was more than a perk—it was tangible evidence that steady effort was rewarded.

The insurance industry would take Geoff far beyond Tasmania. In 1974, he relocated to Western Australia, embracing the uncertainty of change with characteristic calm.

Three years later, he accepted an interstate transfer to Wagga Wagga as Branch Manager. There, he and his wife Noelene built a life over eighteen formative months, before returning west when Geoff was appointed Assistant State Manager.

When the company eventually closed, Geoff faced one of life's inevitable disruptions. True to form, he did not dwell on disappointment. Instead, he adapted. A brief period as a broker confirmed what he already sensed—that his experience and temperament were suited to something more enduring. In 1986, alongside trusted colleague and friend Gerrard McKenna, he co-founded McKenna Hampton Insurance Brokers Pty Ltd.

What began as a calculated leap of faith became the cornerstone of Geoff's professional legacy. Over the next 27 years, the business grew steadily and responsibly. At its peak, it employed 27 staff and operated from its own premises in Ord Street, West Perth. Clients valued the firm not only for technical expertise, but for integrity and genuine care. Staff remained loyal because they were respected. Geoff believed that trust, once earned, was an obligation to be honoured daily.

When the time came, a multinational firm, PSC Insurance Ltd, made an offer to acquire the business.

Geoff recognised it not as an ending, but as a natural progression.

The sale allowed him to retire with pride, knowing he had built something that would endure beyond his direct involvement.

For all his professional success, Geoff never mistook work for life itself. At the centre of everything was family. His marriage to Noelene, spanning nearly 50 years, was the constant anchor of his life. It was a partnership built on affection, mutual respect, and shared values. Together they raised their children and later embraced the joy of grandchildren—a role Geoff approached with quiet delight and unmistakable pride.

He often summed up his philosophy simply: live a good, healthy life; enjoy everything in moderation; and always give your best to your family. Retirement brought the freedom to travel and caravan, but more importantly, it brought unhurried time—time for conversation, laughter, shared meals, and presence. These ordinary moments were, to Geoff, the richest rewards of all.

Alongside family and career, service was the third pillar of Geoff's life. That instinct found its strongest expression through Jaycees, now known as JCI. Joining Launceston Jaycees in 1972, Geoff quickly immersed himself in chapter life, contributing to community projects such as the annual Community Fair.

He discovered in Jaycees a philosophy that resonated deeply: that leadership was best learned through service.

As his career took him to Wagga Wagga, he continued his involvement, helping deliver major fundraising initiatives such as the Bath-Tub Derby and contributing to national programs including *"Mind Your Own Small Business."* When he later settled in Western Australia and joined Hamersley Jaycees in 1979, his leadership capacity became increasingly evident.

Over the following decade, Geoff served as Membership Promoter, Vice President, President, Immediate Past President, and Chairman of the Host Chapter Regional Conference Committee. He also played an active role in the establishment and extension of new chapters, including Serpentine-Jarrahdale Jaycees and West Coast Jaycees.

His focus was always on sustainability—ensuring that organisations were not just enthusiastic, but well-governed and welcoming to new members.

Geoff's influence extended well beyond chapter level. He served as State Membership Officer and as a National Adjudicator for the Youth Speaks for Australia Contest, bringing fairness, encouragement, and high standards to the program.

As Chairman of the Australian Jaycees Supplies Management Committee, he oversaw the production and national distribution of merchandise and publications—work that, while largely invisible, was essential to the organisation's cohesion and identity.

Even after exhausting the formal age limit in 1990, Geoff never truly stepped away. Instead, he became what JCI values most—a mentor. Younger members sought his counsel regularly, including the 2003 National President, who often turned to Geoff to *"pick his brains."* He gave freely of his time, wisdom, and practical support, even making his office boardroom available for meetings of Jaycees, the JCI Senate Group, and The Jaycees Community Foundation Inc.

In 2004, this lifetime of principled leadership was recognised with the awarding of a JCI Senatorship—the organisation's highest honour. It was not bestowed for a single achievement, but for decades of consistent service that embodied every tenet of the JCI Creed.

One of Geoff's most enduring legacies was his 36 years as a Director of The Jaycees Community Foundation (now known as Albany Heritage Foundation Inc). Serving as Secretary for a decade and later as Deputy Chairman, he provided continuity and sound governance. His professional expertise proved invaluable to the Foundation's flagship project, Whale World, as it evolved into Albany's Historic Whaling Station—now an award-winning heritage and tourism attraction of international significance.

His influence extended internationally through his role as an inaugural Board member of The International Learning Foundation, a global education initiative endorsed by JCI.

He supported ILF's educational initiatives such as the second JCI African Academy in Nairobi and a contribution to the JCI Foundation's Phil Pugsley Patron program. In recognition of his service, he was awarded Life Membership of The Jaycees Community Foundation Inc. in 2001.

Running in parallel with his Jaycees commitments was Geoff's deep devotion to Freemasonry. Initiated into the Lodge of Unity No. 11, his Masonic journey spanned nearly four decades. He served in almost every office within the Lodge, including Worshipful Master in 1995 and again in 2014, and Treasurer for an extraordinary 14 consecutive years.

His leadership extended well beyond his Lodge. He held senior offices within the Grand Lodge of Western Australia, including Past Senior Grand Deacon and Past Grand Pursuivant. In Royal Arch Masonry, he was Exalted in 1997 and rose to become Past Deputy Grand Zerubbabel and District Grand Inspector of Workings. His service across the side degrees culminated in his appointment as Deputy Grand Master of the Grand Mark Lodge in 2024.

To his brethren, Geoff was known for quiet authority, deep knowledge, humility, and unwavering fraternity. He led not by force of personality, but by example, patience, and wisdom.

Geoff's commitment to community also extended into sport. He was actively involved and devoted more than a decade to junior Australian Rules football.

From 1992, he gave countless hours to the Carine Junior Football Club, rising to Vice President in 1999 and later serving as Coordinator of Junior Football. Life Membership of the Club stands as testament to the difference he made in the lives of young players and their families.

Sport also remained a personal pleasure—football, badminton, table tennis, golf—and later in life, the shared highs and lows of supporting the West Coast Eagles alongside friends and family.

Geoff approached life's challenges with clarity and calm. When difficulties arose, he assessed them carefully, found practical solutions, and moved forward without fuss. That steady mindset carried him through business, leadership, and family life alike.

His passing was sudden and deeply felt, yet there is comfort in knowing that his life lacked nothing in purpose or contribution. He loved and was loved. He strengthened institutions, mentored future leaders, and left communities better than he found them.

Geoff Hampton's legacy is not confined to titles or honours—though they were many—but to lives touched, opportunities created, and values quietly modelled. It is, in every sense, the story of a mover and shaker who never sought the spotlight, and of a life lived fully, generously, and well.

Fred Harrington OAM

Steady Hands, Quiet Strength

My direct contact with Fred Harrington over the years has been limited, but consistent. Our paths crossed periodically at JCI Australia events, usually because Fred was there as the quiet, steadfast "plus one" supporting his wife Irene—someone I had already come to know well through our shared involvement in Jaycees. Even then, it was apparent that Fred's presence was never incidental. He was observant, engaged and genuinely interested in the people around him, without ever seeking attention.

Over time, it became clear to me that the Harringtons were something rather special. They shared an identical commitment to community and service, yet each pursued that commitment in their own way—sometimes together, often independently, but always with purpose. They are a partnership built not on spotlight or status, but on values, respect and a shared belief that contributing matters. And importantly, they continue to do so.

Like Irene, Fred is very much a quiet achiever.

Fred's ongoing involvement in Probus reflects that same understated dedication.

In May 2021, Fred and Irene were inducted into the Combined Probus Club of St Helena and quickly became active and valued members. Only a few months later, Fred was invited to speak at a monthly meeting, presenting on the Australian Honours system.

Characteristically practical, his focus was not on accolades, but on how to prepare thoughtful and credible nominations—encouraging members to recognise service in others.

By 2025, Fred had taken on the role of Vice President, with responsibility for sourcing guest speakers for each monthly meeting. It was a role well suited to him—connecting people, encouraging participation and ensuring meetings remained engaging and purposeful. In line with club protocol, he will assume the Presidency in March 2026, continuing a pattern that has defined his life: stepping forward when needed, serving diligently, and doing so without fuss.

His contributions are substantial, his influence enduring, yet he remains understated about both. Today, as Chair of the Victoria Branch of the Order of Australia Association, he continues to serve with the same steady, thoughtful approach that has characterised his life.

So before assumptions are made that Fred Harrington's story is simply an adjunct to that of his more publicly visible spouse, it is worth pausing.

What follows is the story of a man whose leadership has been exercised largely behind the scenes, whose impact has been profound rather than loud, and whose life stands as a reminder that some of the most meaningful contributions are made without fanfare. Some people leave their mark not by standing at the front, but by standing firm.

They are the ones who keep systems working, communities functioning and people supported, often without applause or expectation of recognition. Frederick John Harrington is one such man. His life story is not defined by grand gestures or self-promotion, but by consistency, integrity and an unshakeable sense of responsibility—to his work, his family and his community.

Fred Harrington was born on 22 August 1947 in Carlton, Victoria, the first child of George Carpenter Harrington and Yvonne Margaret Harrington (née Dicker). Four years later, his brother Keith arrived, completing a close-knit family. Both parents have since passed, but the values they instilled—hard work, honesty and perseverance—remain deeply woven into Fred's character.

Fred's early schooling began at Holy Spirit Primary School in East Thornbury. He was an above-average student, completing Grades 3 and 4 in a single year, and was tall for his age—a fact that mattered greatly in the playground, where being picked early for football teams carried its own quiet validation. Living only a few hundred metres from the school allowed him to arrive early and stay late, filling his days with cricket, football and the simple joy of being outdoors with friends.

Secondary school at St Joseph's Technical College in Abbotsford proved more challenging. With few familiar faces and the firm discipline of the Christian Brothers,

Fred did not particularly enjoy those years, though he later recognised them as a valuable preparation for adult life. There were, of course, the occasional days when he convinced his mother he wasn't well enough to attend—small rebellions that now bring a wry smile.

Outside school, Fred's childhood and teenage years were rich with freedom and movement. His father bringing home a second-hand bicycle remains one of his fondest memories. That bike opened up a world. School holidays were spent riding with friends, exploring neighbourhoods and gradually pushing boundaries. He joined the Preston and Coburg Pedal Clubs and later the Preston Amateur Cycling Club, competing in both track and road events. On one particularly ambitious holiday, at 14 he rode from Melbourne to Ballarat to visit his aunt—a journey that spoke volumes about his determination long before he recognised it in himself.

Before television arrived in their home, Fred and his brother would regularly walk two kilometres to their grandparents' house just to watch TV. It was never a hardship—just another shared adventure. Those walks quietly reinforced independence, resilience and the understanding that effort was simply part of life.

Academically, Fred completed Year 10 at a higher level, enabling him to begin a Diploma of Civil Engineering at Preston Institute of Technology.

It was the start of a long and occasionally interrupted educational journey. Like many young men, Fred discovered that life offered distractions beyond textbooks. After passing only four first-year subjects, he shifted to night school, balancing work and study from 1964 to 1974. In 1975, he made a decisive commitment—taking a year off work to return to full-time study and complete his qualification at Swinburne College of Technology (now Swinburne University of Technology)

That decision said much about Fred Harrington. When something mattered, he saw it through.

He later completed a Postgraduate Diploma of Municipal Engineering at Warrnambool Institute of Technology (now Deakin University) and undertook further professional development at Mount Eliza Administrative College. Education, for Fred, was never about prestige—it was about competence, responsibility and doing the job properly.

Fred's working life began modestly at Bayley and Grimster, electrical contractors, where he handled administration, invoicing and phones. He then moved to Saxil Tuxen, Surveyors and Civil Engineers, spending considerable time in the field. There, he was mentored directly by Saxil Tuxen himself—then 81 years old—who taught him the fundamentals of preparing base data and plans for civil construction works. It was a formative experience grounded in practical knowledge and respect for craft.

In 1965, Fred joined Knox Shire Council, where he spent six years developing as an engineer alongside his studies. In 1971, he moved to Eltham Shire Council as an Engineering Assistant, eventually reaching the position of Assistant Shire Engineer during his 18 years there. He was frequently entrusted with acting roles, learning to make decisions grounded in clear thinking rather than hierarchy.

One mentor in particular, John Stamp, left a lasting impression. His advice was simple: if a decision needs to be made, think it through, be clear in your rationale, and stand by it. Fred carried that philosophy throughout his career, offering the same trust and support to those he led.

In 1989, Fred took on his first major executive role as Manager of Engineering Operations and Deputy City Engineer at Broadmeadows City Council. Responsible for around 200 staff across multiple service areas, it marked a significant step into senior leadership and exposure to the political and community dimensions of council life.

What followed was a period of adaptability.

Fred held senior roles across several councils, including Darebin, Croydon/Maroondah and Moreland City Council, where he served as Manager of Environmental Engineering from 1995 to 2011 including the role of Executive Officer of the Municipal Emergency Management Planning Committee.

Arriving soon after council amalgamations, he played a key role in unifying staff, managing contractors and maintaining service delivery through uncertainty and restructure.

Two redundancies during his career—one directly linked to amalgamations—were confronting. Initially unsettling, they ultimately reinforced a familiar pattern: acknowledge the difficulty, then plan the way forward.

In 2010–2011, Fred led a comprehensive review of Moreland's waste and recyclimg services, overseeing strategy development, tendering and service transitions. His professional achievements ranged from designing infrastructure to shaping long-term waste, litter and graffiti strategies. Yet Fred never measured success by projects alone. For him, success was also about building teams, guiding staff through change and creating environments where people could grow.

That belief extended into his personal philosophy: be observant, plan ahead, treat others as you would like to be treated, and admit mistakes when they occur. Panic achieves nothing. Thoughtful action achieves much.

Beyond work, Fred has always contributed quietly to his community. He was a member of Eltham Apex Club from 1973 to 1988, becoming a Life Member in 1988. He has been involved with the Eltham Cemetery Trust since 1983 and has served as its Chair since 1991.

Among his proudest achievements there was resolving a long-running land dispute that enabled the cemetery's expansion and the development of areas such as The Terrace, Wisteria Walk and Grevillia Gardens—spaces that honour memory and community.

In 2011, Fred was awarded the Medal of the Order of Australia (OAM) for service to the community of Eltham. Like so much else in his life, the honour was accepted with gratitude rather than fanfare.

Even in formal roles, Fred has never sought distinction; instead, distinction has found him through service.

That same spirit led to his involvement with the Order of Saint John of Jerusalem. Invested in 2019, Fred later accepted appointment—alongside Irene—as Co-Coordinator of the Melbourne Metropolitan Group following its COVID-related recess. Through steady rebuilding and renewed engagement, the group was restored and, in March 2025, inaugurated as the Melbourne Commandery. Fred was installed as Commander and appointed to the Victorian Priory Administrative Council.

It was familiar ground for Fred—quiet leadership, careful rebuilding, and a focus on leaving things stronger than he found them.

Family has always been central to Fred's life.

He and Irene have been married for 55 years, a partnership defined by mutual respect, shared service and unwavering support. Today, time with grandchildren brings particular joy, as does cooking, watching sport and quietly compiling family history.

That history includes deeply personal research into his great-uncle, Frederick John Carpenter, killed on the Western Front in July 1916. Fred has had the family's DNA recorded in the hope his great-uncle's remains may one day be identified and has ensured his story is registered with the Australian War Memorial—an act of remembrance and continuity.

Fred has also faced serious personal challenges, including a diagnosis of prostate cancer in 2012. It reinforced lessons he already understood: life is precious, vigilance matters, and responsibility extends to one's own wellbeing.

If there is one lesson Fred Harrington offers, it is this: leadership is not about control, but trust. Allow people to develop. Give them opportunities. Support their decisions. Stand beside them when things are difficult. Do the work properly and do it with integrity.

In a world often drawn to noise and urgency, Fred Harrington's life reminds us of the enduring power of steady hands, clear thinking and quiet strength. His may not be an ordinary life—but it is an exemplary one.

Irene Harrington OAM

Making Waves and a Better World

It is difficult to pinpoint exactly when I first met Irene Harrington. Like many enduring connections, it didn't arrive with ceremony or announcement—it simply began, quietly, and then stayed. I suspect it was about 1983, a few years before I reached JCI Australia's compulsory retirement age of forty.

At the time, I was privileged to hold the Public Relations role in National President Des Powell's formidable team during the organisation's golden anniversary year in Australia. Among them was Irene, co-opted as National Minute Secretary. Even then, she stood out—not through force of personality or ambition, but through calm competence, warmth and an unmistakable respect for people.

History would later record that Irene went on to become the first female National President of Australia in 1988, hosted the JCI World Congress in Sydney and received another remarkable award. Yet entirely consistent with the woman many of us already knew, she remained steady, principled and deeply people-centred.

Our paths continued to intersect over the years, including in one role we would later share. I was one of Irene's successors as Chairman of the JCI Australia Senate, a body that brings together Senators—Life Members—of the world organisation. By then, professional respect had long since become friendship.

It was therefore a particular pleasure, and a personal honour, when Irene agreed to write the foreword to my book *The MissADVentures of a Hapless Entrepreneur – Timing is Everything*, a work that loosely traces my own business journey.

But titles and shared roles tell only a small part of the story.

What truly sets Irene Harrington apart is not the list of offices held or awards received—impressive though they are—but the way she has lived her life. Quietly. Thoughtfully. With integrity, kindness and an unwavering belief that people matter. She has never sought to lead for the sake of leading, yet leadership has found her time and again. She has never chased recognition, yet recognition has followed service.

Some lives are loud, marked by fanfare and ambition. Others unfold more quietly, guided not by a hunger for recognition but by an unwavering commitment to people, purpose and kindness. Irene Phyllis Harrington's life belongs firmly to the latter. Hers is a story not of chasing titles, but of earning respect; not of seeking the spotlight, but of standing steadily where she was needed most. It is a life lived by a simple but powerful credo: *Don't just float through life—make waves.*

Irene was born on 19 October 1948 in Dundee, Scotland, the second child of Ronald Dickson Smith and Phyllis Fleming Smith (née Low). Her brother Frank arrived a year earlier, and together they formed a small but close-knit family.

When Irene was just three years old, her parents made a decision that would shape not only her life, but generations to follow. With £85 in the bank, a suitcase each, two young children and an extraordinary measure of courage, they emigrated to Australia.

Life in Australia did not begin easily. Financially and emotionally, the early years were tough. There were moments—never spoken of at the time—when her parents feared they might need to place their children in foster care until they could find their feet. Irene only learned this as an adult. What she remembers instead is warmth, laughter and love. She remembers a home where, despite limited means, she never felt deprived.

Her mother Phyllis was a gifted cook, baker and seamstress. Christmas dinner might have been chicken rather than turkey, but it felt special. Clothes were made by hand, often ingeniously fashioned from dyed blankets and finished with fur collars or thoughtful adornments. Irene didn't feel "poor"; she felt cared for. Her father Ronald, apprenticed as a grocer at fourteen, possessed a remarkable mechanical mind. He worked on adding machines, took on multiple jobs when necessary—sometimes three at once—and eventually found stable employment with the local council. Together, her parents modelled resilience, dignity and an extraordinary work ethic.

Though money was scarce, happiness was not.

Holidays were replaced with family picnics. Cinema trips gave way to shared stories and laughter. Irene helped around the house willingly and proudly, learning early that contribution mattered.

Irene's education began at St. Kilda Primary School and continued at Olympic Village Primary School, a place forever etched in her memory. In 1956, the Melbourne Olympic Games came to town, and her school sat right beside the entrance to the athletes' village. She remembers the flags—so many flags—flying behind her class photo, the energy of the comings and goings, and the sense that the world had suddenly arrived at her doorstep. It planted something in her: curiosity, possibility, and a feeling that life extended far beyond her immediate horizon.

She later attended Rosanna High School, where she thrived. Irene loved school—so much so that she never wanted to leave it. She performed consistently well academically, represented her school across multiple sports, and was elected Prefect by both staff and students in her final year. Leadership roles came naturally: sports captain, house vice-captain, and the quiet respect of her peers.

In Year 11, she was awarded a teaching bursary—recognition of both ability and promise. Yet life intervened. Health issues and family finances meant Irene left school to go to work. For years afterward, she would dream of returning to full-time education.

That longing never quite left her, but neither did her love of learning.

Work came early and steadily. Irene began her career in a finance company, working in property and business finance—work she enjoyed, particularly the people. Over time, she held senior administrative roles across private industry and government.

Later, as family life took precedence, she worked part-time roles that allowed her to remain present at home while still contributing professionally.

Marriage brought both partnership and purpose. On 18 April 1970, Irene married Frederick John Harrington—Fred—a man who would become her constant supporter, sounding board and greatest mentor. Their marriage, now spanning fifty-five years, has been marked by shared values, mutual respect and a deep belief in each other's potential. Fred's involvement in Apex opened a new world for Irene: community service, leadership and the profound satisfaction of helping others.

Motherhood, however, did not come easily. For Irene, the journey toward having children was one of the most personally challenging periods of her life.

She had always believed being a mother was her destiny. When that path became uncertain, it tested her deeply.

Yet life, as it often does, offered its gifts in unexpected ways. Irene and Fred adopted a baby girl, and the moment she was placed in Irene's arms remains one of the most magical of her life. Later, they were blessed with a biological son. Together, their children brought joy, growth and—at times—the normal heartaches of parenting. Today, Irene looks at the adults they have become with immense pride, seeing in them compassion, respect and a strong sense of citizenship.

Community involvement became the thread that wove through every stage of Irene's adult life. From Eltham Apex Ladies to Meals on Wheels, sheltered workshops, school councils and parents' associations, Irene gave generously of her time and energy.

Her involvement with Australian Jaycees (JCI Australia), beginning in 1978, proved transformative. What started as a desire to contribute locally evolved into a national and international journey. Irene served on the National Board multiple times and, in 1988, became National President and host for the JCI World Congress in Sydney. She was the first woman to hold the role—but she never wanted that to define her. What mattered more was earning the trust of her peers.

That same year, Irene achieved what she once believed impossible: she was awarded Outstanding National President of the World by Junior Chamber International— the first Australian, and the first woman globally, to receive the honour.

The recognition was profound, not because of prestige, but because it taught her to believe in herself. Her parents' pride meant everything.

Equally meaningful was the lesson she learned from mentors like David Burgess, a past JCI Australia National President. David treated everyone the same—princes, prime ministers and taxi drivers alike. He listened, encouraged and made people feel important. Irene took that lesson to heart, guided by the saying: *"Make me feel important and I won't let you down."* It became central to how she led, worked and lived.

Professionally, Irene's career culminated in what she still describes as her best job: Office Manager for the Geography Teachers Association of Victoria. After ten fulfilling years, a diagnosis of breast cancer forced her to retire from full-time work. Yet even then, she found ways to contribute—working part-time from home as Secretariat Manager for JCI Australia.

In 2008, Irene fulfilled a long-held ambition by becoming a registered Civil Celebrant. It was work that aligned perfectly with who she was: thoughtful, respectful and deeply people-centred. She remains actively involved today, and has served on the National Committee of the Australian Federation of Civil Celebrants since 2012, including as National Vice President, contributing through leadership, writing and advocacy.

Her community service has been extensive and enduring—spanning decades and organisations. From Road Trauma Support Services Victoria (now known as Amber Community), where she served as President, Vice President and Board Member and later became a Life Member, to her role as a Speaker for Cancer Council Victoria's Relay for Life events, Irene's presence has been steady and compassionate. She chaired centenary celebrations for her church, convened national conferences, edited national publications and has served as a Justice of the Peace since 1991.

In May 2021, Irene and Fred were inducted into the Combined Probus Club of St Helena, quickly becoming active participants in the life of the club. For Irene, Probus offered another familiar forum for connection, conversation and shared experience. In April 2025, she was invited to speak at a monthly meeting on the fifty-year history of celebrancy in Australia, weaving history with personal reflection. The response led to further invitations to speak at Probus and VIEW Clubs across the district. As so often in Irene's life, influence flowed not from self-promotion, but from authenticity.

Recognition came in 2016, when Irene was awarded the Medal of the Order of Australia (OAM) for service to the community. The honour mattered deeply—not only for what it represented, but for the joy it brought her friends, whose pride moved her as much as the award itself.

This followed earlier recognition as Outstanding Senator of the World and Life Membership of JCI Australia.

In June 2019, Irene's commitment to service found another expression when she was invested into the Order of Saint John of Jerusalem Knights Hospitaller OSJ–Malta. A Christian-based organisation with origins in Jerusalem in the 11th century, the Order is known today for its charitable and humanitarian work.

For Irene, the invitation was about alignment rather than status. In June 2023, Irene and Fred accepted appointment as Co-Coordinators of the Melbourne Metropolitan Group, which had been in recess since 2020 due to COVID. Through steady leadership, the group was re-energised and fully functional once more. Irene's contribution was recognised with an elevation in rank within the Order.

That work culminated in March 2025 with the inauguration of the Melbourne Commandery, now one of four within Victoria and the largest in Australasia. Irene was installed as Communications Officer and Hospitaller and appointed to the Victorian Priory Administrative Council—roles she approached, as always, not as honours, but as responsibilities.

Yet perhaps one of the most quietly powerful legacies of Irene's life stands just near her home: a local park.

When her children, Alicia and Glenn, noticed the absence of swings and slides, they organised a petition, met with council representatives and helped shape a community space that now hosts parties, school events and countless shared memories. Today it is officially known as Harrington Reserve—a reminder that making waves doesn't require authority, only initiative.

Irene's personal philosophy is simple and profound: *"It must matter that I was here."* She believes in fairness, kindness and treating everyone as an equal. She believes adversity does not define us—our response does. She feels deeply, thinks carefully, and acts with what others have described as a "velvet glove"—firm, considered and compassionate.

Her greatest joys now include time with her grandchildren, whose achievements fill her with pride, and the quiet pleasures of knitting, reading, dinner parties and shared laughter. She still makes waves—just as thoughtfully as ever.

If Irene Harrington's life teaches us anything, it is this: ordinary beginnings can lead to extraordinary impact. Not through force or ego, but through service, persistence and an unshakeable belief in the value of people. She has lived her life ensuring that, when all is said and done, it truly does matter that she was here.

And because of her, the world is undeniably better.

Movers & Shakers – Irene Harrington OAM

Charity Beneficiaries

The following Charities have been nominated to receive a share of the royalties from the sale of this book by the subjects whose stories are featured in it:

Amber Community (Vic)

Australian Junior Chamber Foundation Inc.

BirdLife Australia

Breast Cancer Care (WA)

Cancer Council WA

Fly2Foundation

Free the Hounds Inc

Life Flight Australia (Darling Downs)

Mettle Women Inc.

MND Association (WA)

Red Nose Ltd (SIDS)

Royal Flying Doctor Service (Western Region)

Sea Rescue Tasmania Inc.

Kevin Judge
A Life of Integrity and Service

It is curious how people enter our lives, disappear for decades, and then reappear through circumstances so improbable they feel almost scripted.

I first encountered Kevin Judge in the 1970s, when the accounting firm of which he was a partner audited a company in which I had an interest. It was a professional, unremarkable intersection – the kind you never imagine will matter again.

Many years later, our paths crossed once more, this time through a chain of events so extraordinary that it cemented a long-term friendship and revealed one of the most astonishing professional experiences Kevin would ever recount.

At the time, I was one of two directors representing investors in a syndicate that had pooled funds to back an organic fertiliser business. The opportunity appeared compelling. Demonstration sites were impressive – including Subiaco Oval, where turf growth was nothing short of spectacular – and the product promised both local and international potential.

There was, however, an immediate concern. The principal proponent had previously served a jail sentence for fraud relating to a government tender. Inquiries suggested he had been a convenient scapegoat for others who later claimed collective amnesia.

Believing in second chances – and perhaps ignoring the wisdom of *"once bitten, twice shy"* – we proceeded, carefully structuring protections for our investors.

As part of a joint venture arrangement, $300,000 was advanced to prevent the operating entity from insolvency. Unknown to us at the time, those funds were misappropriated rather than applied to outstanding debts and employee superannuation. Nonetheless, the business moved forward. A capable CEO was appointed, plans were developed, and a promising European joint venture reached Heads of Agreement stage with one of the continent's largest fertiliser manufacturers.

Then, quietly and destructively, the deal was sabotaged from within.

Greed overtook reason. What might have been a shared success became a stalemate. On legal advice, we exercised the debenture we had wisely secured and appointed a Receiver to take control of the business.

The appointment was scheduled for a Friday. Unfortunately, I was attending a funeral 400 kilometres away when events took a dramatic turn.

I received a call informing me that the factory door was locked and the Receiver forcibly prevented from entering. As he attempted to serve his papers, a criminal lawyer - a director nominee of the inventor – stormed out, violently shoved the Receiver backwards into a rose garden, tore his suit and narrowly avoided causing serious injury.

It was an encounter the Receiver, despite a long and distinguished career, had never experienced.

Realising the gravity of his actions, and potential risk of disbarment, the remorseful lawyer abruptly changed course, allowed the Receiver entry and attempted to dismiss the incident as a misunderstanding, promising to repair the damaged suit.

The rest of our team, barred outside, called the police out of concern.

The plan was for the Receiver to return the following Monday.

He never got the chance.

That Saturday night, the factory was subjected to an arson attack. When fire crews attended, they also discovered a cannabis operation behind the premises. Coincidentally – or not – the company's records and stock were the most severely damaged.

The Receiver caught in the middle of this extraordinary implosion was Kevin Judge.

And it is from this moment – amid chaos, integrity tested and professionalism under fire – that his remarkable life story truly deserves to be told.

Some lives are measured by titles, wealth or public recognition. Others are best understood through the quieter, steadier qualities that shape every decision along the way – integrity, curiosity, service and an unwavering commitment to relationships. Kevin Ernest Judge's life belongs firmly in the latter category. It is a life marked not by grand gestures alone, but by consistency of character, generosity of spirit and a belief that effort, when sincerely given, returns rewards far beyond expectation.

Kevin was born on 1 October 1946 in Subiaco, Western Australia, into a lively household already shaped by siblings and shared responsibility. His parents, Alan George Collis Judge and Dorothy May Judge, raised their family with values that would quietly but firmly guide Kevin throughout his life. He arrived into the world as a twin, alongside his sister Sandra Dorothy, joining older siblings Jocelyn Kay and Alan Victor. From early on, Kevin learned the art of coexistence – of listening, negotiating, and understanding that life was rarely about standing alone.

As a boy, Kevin enjoyed school and participated enthusiastically in its opportunities, even if he later described himself as "somewhat, but not overly conscientious." What he lacked in rigid academic discipline, he more than compensated for with engagement and curiosity. He excelled in sport, earning selection in both his high school football and swimming teams, experiences that reinforced teamwork, resilience and the satisfaction of shared success.

One formative moment from his early teenage years would leave an imprint far deeper than any school trophy. At fourteen, working as a paper boy, Kevin stole a chocolate bar from his employer. The proprietor knew – Kevin was certain of it – but never said a word. The silence proved devastating. Overcome with guilt, Kevin internalised a lesson that would shape his moral compass for life. Trust, honesty and integrity were not abstract concepts; they were fragile, precious things, easily damaged and slow to rebuild. From that moment on, integrity ceased to be optional.

Kevin's young adulthood unfolded against the backdrop of global uncertainty. At age twenty, the selection of his birthdate marble meant conscription into the Australian Army and deployment to the Vietnam War. It was an experience that could have derailed a young man's future. Instead, it tempered him. Serving from 1967 to 1969, including a year in Vietnam, Kevin learned discipline, composure under pressure and the importance of staying in control when circumstances threatened to overwhelm. He emerged unscathed physically, but profoundly shaped by the friendships forged under extreme conditions – friendships that endure to this day.

The war left other legacies as well. Kevin found that wherever he travelled in Australia, there was often a veteran connection waiting, a sense that he would be "looked after famously." He also qualified for a war service loan, which would quietly but significantly assist him in building a foundation through real estate investment. Fate, it seemed, had not only tested him but offered tools for rebuilding.

Returning to civilian life, Kevin resumed his professional journey. He began in 1966 as a junior clerk with Dalgety NZL Co, before moving into the accounting profession in earnest. After Vietnam, he joined VK Truman Accountants in Kalgoorlie in 1970, and in 1971 commenced what would become a long and distinguished association with Shepherd & Partners Accountants, later known as Horwath & Horwath. By 1974, Kevin was a partner, a role he would hold until 1988.

Parallel to his professional growth was the most important partnership of his personal life. In 1971, Kevin married Petrice Anne Sutherland, a clinical psychologist whose intelligence, insight and emotional acuity would enrich every dimension of their shared life. Their meeting at the Rottnest Island Hotel, while celebrating the completion of their tertiary studies, changed everything.

When Kevin proposed, Petrice had plans of her own – a European adventure with her girlfriends.

His response was as bold as it was heartfelt: marry me, and I promise we will travel overseas together every year. It was a promise kept. Over the decades, Kevin and Petrice would visit more than 80 countries, many of them repeatedly, shaping a shared life defined by curiosity, culture and connection.

In 1989, Kevin faced one of the most testing professional challenges of his career – a major fallout with business partners. For many, such a rupture might have been career ending. For Kevin, it became an unexpected opportunity. He established a new firm, Judge Constable Chartered Accountants, which he would lead as partner until 2014. The new venture proved far more rewarding and satisfying than what had come before. Looking back, Kevin often reflects that fate lent a hand.

Throughout his career, Kevin's philosophy never wavered: utmost integrity and honesty. He sought not merely to provide accounting services, but to be recognised as a trusted business adviser. His clients were not transactions; they were relationships. This approach was reinforced by his close friendship and partnership with Brian Smith – a man Kevin admired deeply for his sincerity, entrepreneurial spirit and absolute trust-worthiness.

Kevin's leadership extended well beyond his firm.

He was elected WA Chairman of The Institute of Chartered Secretaries in 1989, and WA President of CPA Australia in 2001, representing some 7,500 members. He later served as Chairman of Directors and a non-executive director for numerous ASX listed companies, roles that reflected both professional esteem and personal credibility.

Yet it is perhaps in community service that Kevin's reach has been widest. Over many years, he contributed to fundraising and governance for organisations including the Salvation Army, Red Cross, Motor Neurone Disease, United Way, People Who Care, Clontarf Aboriginal College, Edith Cowan University, the Retina Association, Perth Children's Hospital-and Celebrate WA.

His involvement with the Save the Rhino Foundation was particularly hands on, serving as Treasurer and Vice President for a decade. On one memorable occasion, while distributing goods and spare vehicle parts to Zimbabwean rangers protecting rhinos, Kevin and his companions were thanked with a heartfelt chorus sung by the rangers – enthusiastically, if somewhat inaccurately – of *"God Bless Austria"*.

The moment captured Kevin's enduring delight in human connection, humour and goodwill.

Kevin and Petrice's home life became another powerful expression of their philosophy.

In 1980, when purchasing their Applecross riverfront home, Petrice suggested they forego a holiday house and instead create a resort-like environment at home. The decision proved inspired. Through thoughtful renovations – including pool and tennis court – their home became a gathering place for largescale entertaining.

An antique grand piano acquired with the house, restored and proudly displayed, became the heart of many musical evenings. Kevin's attempt to learn piano under a teacher connected to David and Gillian Helfgott revealed little musical talent, but something far richer followed. The Judges developed a deep friendship with the Helfgotts. Kevin became their accountants. and the couple assumed the role of concert tour managers for seven tours of South Africa and Zimbabwe. These journeys opened the doors to safari life, international audiences and unforgettable experiences, including the filming of the US program *48 Hours* at their home for the Golden Globe announcement of Geoffrey Rush's Best Actor award for *Shine*.

Their home played host to an extraordinary array of guests – cricketers such as Dennis Lillee, Kim Hughes, Bob Massie and Graeme Wood; artists and performers including Lois Maxwell (Miss Moneypenny), Keith Potger (The Seekers) and Sir Tim Rice; Governors of Western Australia John Sanderson, Ken Michael and Malcolm McCusker and numerous politicians including Premier Carmen Lawrence.

Kevin and Petrice's commitment to hospitality became so defining that they were once featured in a Freemason periodical simply as "The Entertainers."

Travel was not always idyllic. In 1993, Kevin and Petrice were mugged in Spain, losing money, passports, credit cards and treasured jewellery.

The ordeal transformed Kevin's approach to travel security but also strengthened international friendships, particularly with Irish colleagues who provided extraordinary assistance. Ireland would become a frequent return destination, and Irish backpackers a familiar presence at their Applecross door.

Kevin's personal habits reflect his wide interests: medieval history classes, cooking, entertaining, collecting antiques, renovating, attending military talks, watching Antiques Roadshow, exercising at the gym and passionately supporting the West Coast Eagles. He reads mostly nonfiction and historical novels, with a particular fondness for *Freedom at Midnight* by Larry Collins and Dominique Lapierre.

Awards have followed quietly but steadily – from home improvement accolades to recognition for pro bono work, fundraising and community contribution. Notable honours include the 2014 Motor Neurone Award for outstanding support and the 2017 Applecross Rotary Community Award.

When adversity arises, Kevin draws on lessons learned long ago: stay calm, stay objective, and don't panic. Military training taught him control; life taught him tolerance. His guiding lesson to others is simple but profound – involve yourself fully in your business and personal life. The rewards will exceed the effort.

Two quotations anchor his worldview.

One, from Robert Browning: *"Ah, but a man's reach should exceed his grasp, or what's a Heaven for?"*

The other, written each year in the back of his diary, from Stephen Grellet: *"I expect to pass through this world but once; any good thing that I can do... let me not defer nor neglect it, for I shall not pass this way again."*

Kevin Ernest Judge's life is not ordinary.

It is a life shaped by integrity, generosity and sustained involvement – in business, in community and in friendship.

Through calm leadership, open doors and an unfailing respect for others, he has shown that a life well lived is not measured by what is accumulated, but by what is shared and the trust that endures long after the work is done.

Seva Mozhaev

From Tokmok to TikTok

Strange how a walk in the park could evolve into an extraordinary story!

As was my habit, it was my turn to take our rescue hound Chevy on his daily expedition to the local park. After half a lap, I noticed an extremely tall (and at 208 cm I do mean tall) young fellow approaching - similarly exercising his accompanying four-legged companion that I came to know was Wilson. Pleasantries exchanged, we continued the conversation as our dogs also enjoyed the company on the final circuit. Also, as is my habit, I presented my business card.

To my surprise, I received an email within a day seeking a cup of coffee and a brief brain-picking - which I am always happy to offer while I am still able.

From our original conversation I was aware of that Seva Mozhaev was a mathematics teacher, but the signature block listed Wedding Photographer, Videographer and Social Media Expert. This, he proclaimed in the email, was a recently acquired passion in the previous two years.

His ultimate aim was to escape the rat race and have a passive income that allowed him to do whatever he liked and that was – "to help people. "

He also confided that while teaching was super rewarding, he wanted more, to scale it to outside the walls of the current education system which, in his opinion, was well out of date.

Always keen to mentor those who have the common sense to learn from others' mistakes, I readily agreed. In the hour or so at the local Dome coffee shop later that week I offered some general advice. It was to be some years later that I was to find out what pearl of wisdom had helped leverage his alternative career.

Having noted the "Social Media Expert" tag, I invited him to participate on a survey of preferred cover of my book series. I did have at the back of my mind that assistance with social media may be handy when the books were to be launched.

With Covid intervening, it was some time before the next connection and, having followed social media posts, I discovered that he had amassed 1.3 million followers on TikTok.

Coincidentally, this was at a time when I was due to co-host a lunch courtesy of a successful bid for a lot in Swan Districts Football Club annual auction. It was for a full three course meal with drinks for 6 or 8 guests in the Parliament House Dining Room.

Donated by the local member, Dave Kelly MLA, it is an enjoyable culinary expedition into the inner sanctum of power that few get to experience.

The TikTok *"millionaire"* was one of my invited guests and, during an entertaining lunch, I was to learn that he had benefited from one concept I had mentioned at our coffee conflab a few years before. When acknowledging that his community involvement was minimal, I had recommended that he seriously consider *"giving back"* to the community in some form - whether that be by membership of a community organisation or other volunteering effort in time or expertise. In my experience, this approach had invariably been repaid in multiples in some form and became a pillar of my philosophy from an early age.

Innovatively, he had applied this *"giving"* principle at a wedding expo by providing all exhibitors with a photograph of their display at no charge. This *"free"* service had seen his wedding photography business booked up for two years. A simple, low-cost marketing strategy that had certainly borne fruit and it was nice to know it worked for him.

As might have been anticipated, the rest of my guests were keen to understand how he had accumulated an increasing number of TikTok followers that had now swelled to 1.6 million.

Being aware of the current obsession of youth with social media on mobile phones that had now encroached into the classroom, he saw this as an opportunity to be exploited. It was a new way to teach mathematics and other lessons – via short entertaining sessions on TikTok - on which he was now a national (and international) sensation.

This really hit home after our enjoyable culinary expedition. As we departed the Parliament House lobby, other guests were staggered to see a flock of primary school children swarm around my towering and youngest guest with multiple requests for selfies. Apart from the puzzled teachers supervising the group tour of state Parliament, another school group were also excitedly pointing to the unmissable TikTok star. Apart from his height, he was instantly recognisable by the younger generation. I was even to discover that my 23-year-old grandson in Melbourne knew of him.

Wow! - the power and impact of social media.

Now, if you search Seva Mozhaev on Google, you will see an array of short clips on Instagram and TikTok. Many are aimed at positively addressing a number of issues affecting young people today – from the dangers of vaping to suicide prevention and mental health – doing a power of good.

The heading of this memoir aptly captures Seva's amazing story.

Seva Mozhaev's journey from the serene mountains of Kyrgyzstan to the vibrant city of Perth, in Western Australia, is a story filled with resilience, determination, and a relentless pursuit of dreams.

Born on January 1, 1991, in the quiet town of Tokmok, Seva's early life was shaped by the deep bond he shared with his mother, Maia Mozhaeva. Though the absence of a known father figure left a void in Seva's life, his mother became his guiding light, instilling in him the confidence to embrace life's challenges head-on.

Growing up, Seva found solace in nature, particularly in the rugged mountains of Russia, where he spent cherished moments fishing and hunting with his grandfather. These experiences nurtured in him a love for the outdoors and provided a sense of calm amid the challenges of his childhood. Alongside his sibling Que, Seva navigated the complexities of a childhood without a strong father figure but found strength in his family, especially in the resilience of his mother.

When his family relocated to Kalgoorlie, a gold-mining town in Western Australia, Seva's life took a significant turn. Adjusting to a new culture and environment was challenging, but it was in Kalgoorlie that Seva began to shape his future.

He was a curious student, always questioning, always seeking more.

While his thirst for knowledge and fueled his love for learning, Seva often found himself frustrated with the rigidity of traditional education. He enjoyed some parts of school, but many aspects left him feeling unfulfilled, longing for a deeper sense of purpose.

Seva's passion for sports, particularly Australian Rules Football (AFL), became his outlet. Upon completing high school, Seva moved to Perth in 2009 at the age of 19, determined to pursue his AFL dream. He played for both Subiaco and West Perth in the WA Football League, driven by his love for the game and the thrill of competition. Yet, Seva's journey in football, like many of his endeavours, was not without its challenges. Balancing his athletic pursuits with work, he took on roles as a pool and beach lifeguard and even tried his hand at labouring in door and window manufacturing. Each job, while not his passion, contributed to his growing understanding of discipline and perseverance.

His passion for fitness led him to a career as a personal trainer, a role that allowed him to guide others on their physical journeys. Seva enjoyed helping people achieve their health goals, and soon, he was operating his own personal training business out of his home, preferring a private, low-overhead setup. During this period, he also pursued a Bachelor of Secondary Education at Edith Cowan University (ECU), inspired by his mother's career as a teacher.

Specialising in Physical Education and Science, Seva quickly found his footing in the world of education and, against all odds, landed a permanent full-time position as a mathematics teacher right out of university—an uncommon achievement for a first-year graduate.

But Seva's ambitions were never confined to the classroom. In 2019, a side hustle that had started as a hobby—photography—began to flourish. What started as capturing moments for friends quickly transformed into a wedding photography business. His entrepreneurial spirit kicked in, and Seva turned his passion into a thriving business. By 2021, he had made the bold decision to step away from teaching and dedicate himself entirely to photography and his growing online presence.

Seva's ability to leverage social media, particularly TikTok, skyrocketed his business. He built a following of over 1.6 million people, using his platform to share not only his photography but also his insights on digital marketing and business growth. His online success paved the way for a consulting and advisory career, where he now teaches other businesses how to harness the power of social media to grow their brands.

Through it all, Seva credits much of his success to the influence of his mother, Maia. She taught him resilience, self-confidence, and the importance of breaking cycles of limitation.

Seva's admiration for his mother runs deep, recognising her sacrifices and strength as the foundation upon which his own self-belief is built.

Today, Seva is a man who wears many hats. He is a successful entrepreneur, educator, and social media influencer, but most importantly, he is someone who has taken control of his time and destiny. His philosophy is simple yet powerful: there is more to life than just going through the motions. For Seva, true success lies in helping others realise their potential and guiding them toward a more meaningful, fulfilling path.

Seva's story is not without setbacks, but each obstacle has only fuelled his determination to succeed. From being kicked out of university due to a misunderstanding with a mentor—a decision he fought and had overturned—to juggling multiple jobs while pursuing his dreams,

Seva's journey is a testament to resilience and the power of self-awareness. He has learned that adversity is simply an opportunity to learn something new, a chance to pivot, and a moment to grow stronger.

One of Seva's greatest accomplishments has been booking his wedding photography business two years in advance, a testament to his work ethic and talent. But perhaps his most rewarding success is the impact he's had on others.

Seva's goal is to shake hands with countless individuals who can look him in the eye and say, *"You helped me find my path."*

When he's not working or creating content, Seva finds peace in walking his dog with his wife, Sabine, to whom he is happily married. Together, they enjoy camping trips to Margaret River, where they can disconnect and enjoy nature. Snowboarding, too, remains a dream for Seva—one he hopes to indulge in a few times a year with his growing family.

In the end, Seva's journey is far from over. He continues to push boundaries, challenge norms, and inspire others to do the same. Whether it's through his photography, his teaching, or his consulting work, Seva Mozhaev is living proof that with self-awareness, resilience, and a willingness to pivot, anyone can achieve their dreams.

And for Seva, the greatest lesson he can share is this: the most important thing you can do is buy your time back. To live life on your terms is the ultimate freedom, and through his own story, Seva empowers others to strive for that same independence. As he moves forward, Seva remains committed to helping others discover their potential and guiding them on their journey to success.

Carmelo Musca

From Weddings to Film-Maker

With the passing of time, it is hard to remember exactly when or how I first met Carmelo Musca. But it was in early 1981, when the Australian Government—eager to support the nation's film industry—introduced a tax incentive for investment in Australian filmmaking.

For every dollar invested, a tax deduction of $1.50 could be claimed, and only half of the income from the film was taxable. Eventually, the Government realised the scheme was costing more than expected, reducing the deduction to $1 per $1 invested. This successful program, which helped develop Australia's film industry, continued until 2007, when it was replaced by the Producer Offset.

At the time, I was working in the tax-effective investment and project syndication sector. Our Italian corporate lawyer introduced me to a young Sicilian wedding photographer who, having dabbled in a few early documentaries, was eager to pursue filmmaking as a career.

I, meanwhile, was absorbed in a different kind of community project—the restoration of Australia's last derelict whaling station in Albany, Western Australia. It had been gifted to the Foundation I chaired, and we had ambitious plans to turn it into a viable tourist attraction—a goal we successfully realised over the next 40 years. But that's a story for another time.

Back to the aspiring filmmaker: with some creative thinking, we approached my network of contacts, many of whom were interested in supporting the arts but were also motivated by the idea of gaining a tax deduction roughly equivalent to their normal tax liability, with the possibility of a 50% tax-free return if the project succeeded.

For me, it was an ideal opportunity to have the story of the whaling station captured for posterity, funded by third parties, and screened in the museum theatre. This became one of six documentaries produced by Carmelo through his CM Films Productions, for which we arranged funding.

In truth, we may have inadvertently changed his career path—from still photographer to international film producer. Amazing how fate works.

And yes, *"Albany Whaling"* chronicled Western Australia's whaling industry from its beginnings, long before wheat and wool, right through to its closure in November 1978. The world premiere was attended by the State Minister for Tourism, screening with another of Carmelo's productions—*"I Am No God"*, a documentary about West Australians visiting a faith healer in the Philippines. Despite the blood and gore of the faith healer scenes, it was the whale processing that had the Minister dry-reaching—a moment I jokingly reminded him of more than 40 years later.

As a postscript, that half-hour television documentary won an international award—Carmelo's first. It is still for sale in the old whaling station gift shop, with all proceeds going to the museum.

Born in 1951 in the picturesque town of Sinagra, Sicily, Carmelo Nunzio Musca entered the world as a child of promise and resilience. The eldest of Angelo and Domenica Musca's children, he grew up surrounded by values of hard work, humility, and generosity—principles that laid the foundation for a life filled with triumphs, challenges, and a commitment to making a difference.

In early childhood, Carmelo moved with his family to Bayswater, Western Australia. Adjusting to life in a new country was not without challenges. At St. Columbus Catholic Primary School, he faced the daunting task of learning English while navigating a new culture. By the time he attended Bayswater State School, he was thriving academically and socially. Cricket became a cherished part of his daily routine, symbolising his growing sense of belonging.

Yet, not all memories were golden. Carmelo endured bullying and physical abuse in his early school years—experiences he later transformed into a wellspring of empathy and resilience. These adversities shaped his lifelong belief in treating others with kindness and respect.

Even as a primary school student, Carmelo's creativity shone. At the Maylands Meccano Club, he built cranes, Ferris wheels, and working model cars. He developed his first black-and-white film and made contact photo prints by exposing them to sunlight on photographic paper. He sold his first photograph in Grade 6 and by 17 had his first full colour cover photo on a national magazine – *Hoofs & Horns*.

High school only deepened his passion. He bought his first enlarger and turned the family laundry into a makeshift darkroom. At 16, he purchased a clockwork 8mm movie camera, producing family dramas—his brother as a monster attacking their mother, and Carmelo "rescuing" the babysitter. The unintended smiles on his amateur cast transformed the thriller into his first silent film comedy.

Carmelo attended Cyril Jackson, Kewdale, and Kent Street High Schools, where he discovered an aptitude for mathematics and science. Despite struggles with English, he persevered, matriculating as the first in his extended family to attend university. At the Western Australian Institute of Technology (now Curtin University), he pursued accounting, demonstrating relentless commitment to personal growth and education.

Carmelo's school and university years were characterised by a remarkable work ethic. From selling newspapers at age 12 to cleaning racehorse stables at dawn, he embraced every job with enthusiasm. These experiences not only funded his education but also instilled versatility and resilience that would define his career.

In 1971, Carmelo met Margaret (Maggie) Moynihan in the Fine Art Department darkroom, where she was a student. They married in 1975, embarking on a lifelong partnership built on love, respect, and shared dreams. Together, they raised four children—Michael, David, Lucy, and Nicholas—and later welcomed seven grandchildren. Family became Carmelo's greatest source of joy and inspiration, motivating him to create a legacy of integrity and generosity.

Carmelo's passion for storytelling led him to filmmaking, where he discovered the power to connect with people and inspire change. Over the years, he produced documentaries, promotional films, and feature-length projects that captured the human experience and celebrated cultural diversity.

Under the Australian Government's 10BA film funding scheme, Carmelo produced several acclaimed works, including the feature *"Zombie Brigade"* and numerous documentaries broadcast both domestically and internationally. He directed *"Through Foreign Eyes"*, celebrating the sister-city relationship between Western Australia and Zhejiang Province in China, and co-directed the Chinese-language feature *"Deep Sleep No More"*, premiering at CinefestOZ with some of the Chinese cast in attendance.

One of his most significant projects, *"My Asian Heart,"* screened at the Sydney and Melbourne Film Festivals and won the prestigious ATOM Award as Australia's Best Documentary Film. It chronicled the work of Australian photojournalist Philip Blenkinsop, whose images highlighted human rights issues across Asia. The project demanded both technical skill and emotional sensitivity, navigating complex political contexts to tell a story with integrity.

Carmelo's responsiveness to social issues was also evident in his documentary on the 1976 Italian earthquake. Extensive research and collaboration with relief organisations led to a film that raised over a million dollars for disaster relief.

The people of Gemona in Friuli, Italy, expressed their gratitude by inviting him back in 2006 for the thirtieth anniversary, presenting him with an award, and including him in the launch of the city's film archive—an experience highlighting the transformative power of storytelling.

Educational and cultural films were also central to his work. In 1988, *"Didgeridoo in Deutschland"* followed Indigenous Australian musician Richard Walley performing with the East Berlin Philharmonic Orchestra.

The film captured a historic moment—one of the first times an Aboriginal artist received flowers and a standing ovation on stage in East Berlin. It aired on SBS prime time and continues to be used in schools and cultural education programs.

Another standout was *"The Habits of New Norcia,"* exploring the history of the Benedictine mission in Western Australia. Through meticulous attention to detail, the film brought the spiritual and cultural complexities of this historic institution to life, fostering understanding and appreciation.

Carmelo stresses that filmmaking is a team effort, and while he is only one member of the crew, his skill in deal-making and creative funding ensured these films were realised when others had struggled to secure initial support.

Carmelo's work expanded globally. His 13-part series on artist Andrew Rogers took him to Iceland, Kenya, Namibia, and Antarctica, documenting monumental land art installations while blending stunning visuals with narratives about human connection and environmental stewardship.

Artistic highlights also include the video installation *"Collision Course,"* created with the Australian Dance Theatre and projected internationally in galleries and festivals.

A self-described travel junkie, Carmelo's adventures spanned continents. In 1977, Filmwest/Musca was the only film entity to cover the London-to-Sydney Rally from start to finish—a gruelling 30,000 km journey through Europe, Turkey, Iran, Afghanistan, India, and beyond. Using hire cars, rally cars, helicopters, and light planes, the film *"Imagine Seeing the Cars Going Past"* captured the drivers' personalities and sold to the ABC and BBC.

One iconic moment saw Carmelo ask rally Jeep drivers to drive up the Sydney Opera House steps—a triumphant image encapsulating the spirit of the event.

The production almost didn't happen; filming was called off three days before the start. Carmelo secured two US sponsors at 3 a.m. the Wednesday before the rally, and by 7 a.m., cheques were handed over at The Dorchester in London—just hours before the rally began.

Timing, indeed, is everything.

In 1998, Carmelo read Elisabeth Luard's book "*European Peasant Cookery*." Tracking her down to Mull in Scotland, he co-wrote, directed, and shot the 13-part series *"The Rich Tradition"* with Elisabeth as presenter. The series explored peasant culture, history, and food across 13 European locations—long before Rick Stein or Jamie Oliver popularised such subjects.

It addressed sustainability and environmental issues over 30 years ago and sold to the BBC, SBS, and worldwide.

Carmelo's commitment to community is unwavering. He volunteers his skills to young filmmakers, aspiring artists, and charitable organisations.

His short drama *"See How They Run"* brought attention to disability services, and his involvement with Lions Miss Personality and Miss Charity events showcased his dedication to empowering others.

As a mentor, he guides emerging directors on their first network series, provides equipment and expertise at no cost, and helps writers and musicians create promotional reels. Many of his mentees credit his generosity and wisdom as pivotal to their careers.

It was no surprise then, that Carmelo received the Lotterywest Award for Outstanding Contribution to the Industry at the 2010 West Australian Screen Awards.

Life's challenges have been met with Carmelo's resilience and optimism.

The loss of his brother Alberto to cancer at 34, followed by his father's death ten months later, was profoundly impactful. Yet he found solace in honouring their memories through his work and family life.

When faced with setbacks in filmmaking, he adopts a pragmatic, forward-looking mindset:

"Not getting every project up is not really a failure; you move on to the next one after giving it your best shot."

Carmelo's guiding philosophy is simple:

"Be a good person and treat others as you wish to be treated."

His grandmother's wisdom—*"Love without backbone has no validity"*—is central to his approach, balancing kindness with strength.

Carmelo Musca's life is a testament to resilience, creativity, and generosity. From a young immigrant boy overcoming language barriers in Bayswater to an award-winning filmmaker and global adventurer, he has inspired countless individuals to pursue their dreams.

Through films, community work, and dedication to family, Carmelo leaves an indelible mark. His story reminds us that success is measured not only by accolades but by the lives we touch and the legacy we leave.

As Carmelo advises:

"Have fun, be silly sometimes, and always give your best."

Charity Beneficiaries

The following Charities have been nominated to receive a share of the royalties from the sale of this book by the subjects whose stories are featured in it:

Amber Community (Vic)

Australian Junior Chamber Foundation Inc.

BirdLife Australia

Breast Cancer Care (WA)

Cancer Council WA

Fly2Foundation

Free the Hounds Inc

Life Flight Australia (Darling Downs)

Mettle Women Inc.

MND Association (WA)

Red Nose Ltd (SIDS)

Royal Flying Doctor Service (Western Region)

Sea Rescue Tasmania Inc.

Alan Nelson

Setting Personal Challenges

An unsolicited email targeting senior management of not-for-profits in the northern suburbs of Perth appeared in my inbox. It was an invitation from the Fortuna Foundation to attend a breakfast meeting of leaders of local charities. I quickly understood that it was seeking advice from the third sector, which was of more interest than the offered coffee and Danish pastries.

Fortuna, founded by an accounting and financial advisory group of similar name was looking to reshape its purpose and better understand the changing needs of not-for-profits in an increasingly congested landscape.

A diverse group of CEOs and founders attended, and a detailed follow-up email I sent afterwards prompted further consultation.

With a lunch at Parliament House imminent—courtesy of a successful bid at the annual Swan Districts Football Club auction—I extended invitations to several founders and chairs of charities.

For many, lunch in the State Parliament dining room is a rare and memorable experience and a small reward for community contribution.

One of my seven invitees was Fortuna's founder, who enquired whether his chairman might also attend.

Fortuitously, a prior commitment freed up a seat.

That unexpected guest was Alan Nelson—and within minutes of conversation, it was clear that his life had been shaped by a pattern of deliberate self-challenge rather than conventional comfort.

Alan James Nelson was born on 11 July 1953 in Newcastle, England, into a modest working-class family. His parents, James and Vera, were practical, hardworking people who expected effort, resilience, and self-reliance from their children. Alan was the second of four siblings, with an older sister, Jane, and two younger sisters, Louise and Rachel.

His childhood was not an easy one, and one moment in particular lodged deeply. At the age of eleven, Alan failed the government's 11-plus examination and was sent to what was widely regarded as the "loser" school. On his first day, the teacher asked students receiving free school meals to stand. Only two boys did. Alan was one of them. The silence was deafening. The embarrassment burned.

That moment became a private line in the sand. Alan made a vow he never spoke aloud: *"I will never be poor."*

Years later, he would learn that memory is not always an accurate historian. A former schoolmate laughed when Alan suggested they'd both been driven by that humiliation. *"You were always driven,"* he said. *"You were always working two or three jobs."*

Whether born of circumstance or instinct, effort became Alan's default setting.

School offered both refuge and opportunity. Mischievous, quick-witted, and socially adept, Alan enjoyed learning and thrived in the classroom. Education in the UK was free, and despite early labelling, he progressed well enough to attend university on a full government grant.

He graduated with a degree in Political Economy—wryly observing at the time that it was of limited practical value. In hindsight, it shaped how he understood systems, incentives, power, and human behaviour—foundations that would underpin his leadership decades later.

Curiosity and restlessness soon pulled him beyond the UK. Alan worked in Canada before travelling through the United States, Central America, and South America. For eighteen months, he took whatever work he could find—linesman, concreter, dishwasher, roof tiler, bulldozer driver. It was a grounding education, one that instilled deep respect for people who work hard without recognition or status.

Titles, he learned early, mattered far less than contribution.

Returning to the UK, Alan entered the corporate world, and advancement came quickly—perhaps too quickly. He rose through senior roles faster than experience justified, propelled by confidence and hunger.

The defining break came in 1983 when a failing Middle Eastern business needed one final attempt at survival. No one else wanted the role. At 29, Alan became General Manager and Managing Director.

Through relentless effort, good timing, and a willingness to confront complexity, the business turned around and became highly profitable. His reputation was established. Yet he left after two years, aware—perhaps subconsciously—of the danger of mistaking success for wisdom. He was still proving something, largely to himself.

Senior roles followed across manufacturing and construction-related industries. Confidence tipped into arrogance, though insecurity lingered beneath the surface. Wisdom, as Alan would later reflect, lagged achievement.

Australia offered a circuit breaker. Drawn by lifestyle, climate, and the chance to raise a family, Alan arrived in Melbourne on a Tuesday, secured employment by Friday, and commenced a senior role the following Monday. In 1988, a daughter was born. Soon after, the family moved to Western Australia, where their son arrived two years later.

Professionally, these were demanding years. Alan managed well-known WA companies, including Bristile and Joyce, and was frequently tasked with restructuring troubled businesses. Making people redundant was the hardest responsibility of all.

He recalls thinking repeatedly, *"There must be a better way."* At the time, he didn't yet know what that way looked like.

The pivot came unexpectedly.

An Irish engineer stopped him in a corridor and suggested he attend a leadership course. Alan bristled—hadn't he already attended elite management programs in Europe? Still, he invited the man into his office. What followed was honest, unfiltered feedback. Alan listened—slowly, carefully.

That conversation led him to a Master of Leadership program developed by Professor Ron Cacioppe. It was confronting. Gradually, Alan recognised that leadership was not about intellect or authority, but self-awareness, presence, and impact. It permanently altered how he saw himself and others.

In 1996, leadership was tested in the most confronting way possible. A major accident in his business resulted in loss of life. The responsibility was crushing. In the aftermath, someone said to him, *"A leader sees wellness when there is illness."* Alan realised that until he addressed his own wellbeing, the organisation could not heal. That insight reshaped how he led—and how he lived.

Approaching 45, Alan knew he did not want to remain a corporate employee indefinitely.

Around that time, he set himself a seemingly unrelated challenge: to compete in the Avon Descent, a 144-kilometre white-water race over two days. He wrote it on his whiteboard. If he finished, he would resign.

For six months, he trained relentlessly. On race day, he scraped through each cut-off by minutes. He crossed the finish line with six minutes to spare.

On Monday, he resigned.

With partners, Alan established a railway services business that grew from a single customer into a national operation, eventually employing more than 400 people and reaching turnover of $65 million. Early threats from a dominant customer only sharpened his resolve. Diversification followed. Growth accelerated.

Alan competed in the Avon Descent for a decade, from 1998 to 2008, returning year after year not for medals, but for what the race demanded—discipline, preparation, and the willingness to *dig deeper*.

At 50, he climbed Mount Kilimanjaro. The final ascent was brutal, made harder by the realisation that the summit was followed by eight hours of descent. Endurance, he learned, is often required *after* success. The climb coincided with the end of his first marriage—a chapter he reflects on with honesty and regret, particularly for the impact on his children.

Life, however, proved generous again. Alan later met Jacqui, and together they blended their families—two children each—into a lively, chaotic, deeply loving household. All four children celebrated their 21st birthdays there and fell in love under that roof.

Physical challenge remained a constant. Alan climbed Mount Fuji, Kota Kinabalu, Everest Base Camp, Six Peaks, and many others. He hiked the 1,000-kilometre Bibbulmun Track and rode the 1,000-kilometre Munda Biddi Trail by mountain bike.

These were not acts of bravado, but personal negotiations with endurance, patience, and self-belief.

Today, relaxation looks quieter—long walks, working on renovations at a country property, and time spent reading. His bookshelves lean toward historical and non-fiction works, with favourite authors including James Michener, Ken Follett, Robert Harris, Ben Macintyre, Max Hastings, Matthew Reilly, and Larry Collins. Book clubs and wine clubs provide conversation and connection; once, there was even a Jaguar club.

Awards followed success—Fine Dining, Tourism, Export, and others—but they have never defined him. Community involvement has been limited, though mentoring has become central. Alan now chairs, advises, and supports entrepreneurs and business owners, offering something far more valuable than theory: lived experience.

"The greatest joy I get at this stage of life," he says, *"is helping people."*

He has attempted retirement four times since the age of 54 and failed each time. To slow himself down, he walked the Camino Francés—770 kilometres across northern Spain—finding the journey unexpectedly emotional. Along the way, he listened to *How Not to Be a Grumpy Old Bugger*, which turned out to be more profound than anticipated.

Now, Alan measures life with three simple questions:
Did I enjoy my day?
Did I help someone?
Did I eat healthily?

He is writing a book of short reflections—31 liners with stories attached—distilling decades of mistakes into practical wisdom. His guiding belief is disarmingly simple:

"I have made all the mistakes you can possibly make—and therefore I know what not to do."

Alan Nelson's life has been shaped by adversity, ambition, missteps, and self-imposed challenges. His response to difficulty has always been the same: *"dig deeper."* The Swedish word *"lagom"* resonates with him now—a state of balance, enoughness, and contentment.

He is still setting personal challenges. They are simply measured differently today.

Charity Beneficiaries

The following Charities have been nominated to receive a share of the royalties from the sale of this book by the subjects whose stories are featured in it:

Amber Community (Vic)

Australian Junior Chamber Foundation Inc.

BirdLife Australia

Breast Cancer Care (WA)

Cancer Council WA

Fly2Foundation

Free the Hounds Inc

Life Flight Australia (Darling Downs)

Mettle Women Inc.

MND Association (WA)

Red Nose Ltd (SIDS)

Royal Flying Doctor Service (Western Region)

Sea Rescue Tasmania Inc.

Mette Nielsen

The Nordic Cracker Queen – Life is for Living

The Jaycees Community Foundation Inc began life as a bold and uniquely Western Australian initiative – a spin-off from the state organisation of Junior Chamber International, now known simply as JCI. Established in 1976, the Foundation was governed by a Board drawn from current members of local chapters and Senators (life members) of the international movement. Embedded in its Constitution was a simple but powerful requirement: the serving State President would take a seat at the Board table for their year of office, ensuring continuity between leadership, service and vision.

One such appointment was that of Mette Fraas Nielsen, then a relatively new arrival to Australia.

What could have been a brief, formal contribution became something far more significant. Mette was keen to remain involved beyond her presidential year and, to my great delight as Chairman of the Board, she did exactly that – continuing her service for a further twelve years. For half of that time, she also took on the vital role of Strategic Planning Chairman.

Her professional background as a corrosion engineer proved invaluable at a critical moment in the Foundation's history.

The Foundation had taken on an ambitious and deeply symbolic project: the restoration of Australia's last derelict whaling station.

On the shores of King George Sound in Albany, Western Australia, an abandoned whale chaser and a rusting factory stood as stark reminders of another era. Transforming them into a living, breathing heritage tourist attraction would require vision, resolve – and technical expertise.

Mette brought all three.

Yet even as she quietly contributed to the shaping of one of the Foundation's most important community achievements, a larger question lingered.

What is her story?

There are lives that unfold according to a careful plan, and there are lives that are shaped by curiosity, courage and a willingness to say yes before the full picture is clear.

Mette Fraas Nielsen's story belongs firmly in the second category. It is a story of movement – across countries, careers and cultures – and of a woman who has never allowed circumstance, convention or fear to dictate the limits of her life.

Born on 14 March 1966 in the small Danish town of Ørsted, Mette grew up grounded in family, work ethic and quiet strength. Her parents, Grete Fraas Nielsen and Tage Agerholm Nielsen, shaped her early understanding of what mattered. Her father ran his own business, modelling independence, kindness and the dignity of honest work.

Her mother led by example as a strong, capable woman at a time when equality was often spoken about but not always practised.

While Denmark had achieved genuine gender equality in many professions and education, Mette would later find that this was far from universal. The lessons she absorbed at home would guide her through engineering environments that remained male-dominated in many of the countries where she worked, as well as through the uncertainties of entrepreneurship.

She shared her childhood with an older brother, Esben, born in 1964, and some of her fondest memories come from summer holidays spent with cousins – long, carefree days that seemed to stretch endlessly under Nordic skies. Those summers became touchstones of warmth and belonging, memories she would return to mentally during far more demanding chapters of her life.

Not all memories were easy. One moment, in particular, left a lasting imprint.

As a child, Mette watched her family farm burn down. There was no dramatic heroism in the moment – just the stark helplessness of witnessing something precious disappear in flames. It was a harsh early lesson in impermanence, and perhaps the first time she understood that life could change in an instant.

Years later, that same understanding would underpin her philosophy of living fully and without regret.

From the very beginning, Mette was a keen and diligent student. She spent nine years in elementary school in Auning, followed by three years of high school in Randers, choosing a mathematical and technical line that reflected both her aptitude and her enjoyment of structured problem-solving.

She liked school. She liked learning. Most of all, she liked getting the job done.

That clarity of purpose carried her into higher education, where she trained as a Chemical and Materials Science engineer in Esbjerg.

Engineering, particularly at that time, was not a field overflowing with women. Mette noticed this, but she never allowed it to become a barrier. Her approach was pragmatic and quietly principled: if you want to be treated as part of the majority, there is no room for special treatment. Competence, preparation and integrity would speak louder than protest.

Her professional life began to take on an international shape in the early 1990s.

From 1991 to 1994 she worked as an engineer in Aberdeen, Scotland.

Those years were formative, not just technically but personally. Donald Smith, her first engineering boss, gave her something invaluable – a chance. He trusted her to show what she could do and taught her the fundamentals of business management that would later prove just as important as any engineering equation.

From Scotland, Mette moved to Great Yarmouth and Norwich between 1994 and 1996, before returning to Aberdeen for another year.

Each move required adaptation – new workplaces, new accents, new expectations – and each strengthened her confidence that she could land on her feet anywhere. By 1997, her journey brought her much further south, to Perth, Western Australia.

Perth would become her next home for nearly thirty years. Professionally, Mette thrived, but the period was not without its challenges. The engineering world remained demanding and, at times, unforgiving.

During this chapter she experienced a profound episode of stress, depression and anxiety – a "deepest, darkest pit," as she later described it. It was a sobering moment of reckoning.

One person who made an enormous difference during that time was Simon Bingham, her engineering boss in Perth. Rather than seeing only diminished capacity, he saw potential.

He allowed Mette to do things her way, trusted her judgement and, most importantly, believed in her when she struggled to believe in herself. His support did not erase the difficulty, but it helped her emerge with a clearer sense of what – and who – deserved her energy.

Another challenge had been present since infancy. As a baby, Mette lost the eyesight in one eye. It forced her, from the very beginning, to find ways to see the world differently – quite literally. Rather than limiting her, this early adversity became part of her resilience. She learned to adapt, compensate and focus on what she could do, not what she could not.

Alongside her professional life, Mette was deeply involved in Junior Chamber International (JCI), from 1997 to 2004 in Scotland and Australia, and later through The Jaycees Community Foundation in Perth. JCI opened doors that went far beyond networking. It offered leadership, training, global friendships and a chance to test herself on an international stage.

Her achievements within JCI were extraordinary.

She became a finalist in the World Public Speaking competition in 2001, was elected Australian Junior Chamber (now JCI Australia) National President in 2003, and received many awards at local, state, national, area and international levels.

She also served on The Jaycees Community Foundation Board for thirteen years and played a role in the history-making work around Albany's Historic Whaling Station. Through JCI, Mette discovered the power of community, service and collective ambition.

One influence from that world stands out strongly in her story. The author, then Chairman of The Jaycees Community Foundation, shone a beacon into the possibilities of community involvement. He showed, by example, that nothing is impossible when vision is matched with commitment. That belief would echo later in Mette's entrepreneurial leap.

In 2012, another significant change arrived. Mette married David Cullen, a partner who would become her greatest personal supporter. David's belief in her was unwavering. Flexible, creative and solution-focused, he stood beside her through bold ideas and big transitions, always willing to find a way forward together.

That same year, Mette took a career break to accompany David to live in Beijing, China, during his overseas posting that would last two and a half years. Beijing was confronting, energising and transformative. Immersed in a vastly different culture, she had space to step back and reassess her life. Away from familiar routines, she asked herself a simple but profound question: what do I really want to do?

The answer was entrepreneurship.

She decided to give herself permission to try – properly, wholeheartedly – to create something of her own.

From that decision, *"Mette Is Baking"* was born in 2015. Starting from nothing, she set out to build not just a business, but the best business she possibly could.

What followed was a remarkable decade of creativity, discipline and success. Drawing on her engineering precision, Scandinavian heritage and love of craft, Mette developed a range of baked products that quickly gained attention for their quality and originality. Her Nordic crackers, gluten-free lines and distinctive dip mixes stood out in a crowded market.

The awards soon followed – not one or two, but dozens. Between 2018 and 2024, her products collected an extraordinary tally: 37 food awards across just six products in seven years. These included Champion Trophies, Reserve Champion awards, Best in Class honours, and a cascade of Gold, Silver and Bronze medals from prestigious fine food competitions across Australia.

Her Nordic Crackers won the Australian Food Award Champion Trophy. Gluten-free products earned multiple Champions and Reserve Champions. Dip mixes with evocative names like Scandi Summer, Hygge Mix, Pikant and Viking Herbs captured judges' attention and palates alike.

The consistency of recognition spoke to something deeper than novelty – it reflected rigour, passion and relentless attention to detail.

Commercially, the business flourished. *"Mette Is Baking"* was never in the red. It employed staff, supplied around 50 gourmet stores and built a brand strong enough that, in 2025, Mette sold the business to a major bakery. Crucially, the new owners chose to retain the Mette is Baking branding – a testament to the value she had created.

Along the way, Mette was recognised beyond food awards.

She was named in WA Business News' 40 under 40 in 2006, became a Telstra Business Awards nominee in 2019, and won multiple small business awards, including Best Home-Based Business and a Marketing Award.

In 2021, she was a finalist in the Australian Small Business Champion Awards in the Bakery category.

Despite her achievements, Mette has never defined success narrowly. For her, success also includes living in multiple countries, learning new languages, building social circles from scratch, and being a good friend. It includes becoming a grandmother, despite never having children of her own – a role she embraces with joy and gratitude.

When she relaxes, Mette turns to craft – dressmaking, knitting, crocheting – often creating her own designs.

There is a pleasing symmetry in this: the same hands that once worked through engineering problems now shape fabric and dough, logic and creativity intertwined.

She is drawn to water, finding calm by or in it, and reads selectively, favouring personal development books that encourage reflection over perfection.

Her personal and business philosophies are elegantly simple. *Life is for living. Don't let work get in the way of a great life. Set goals, dream annually, and take opportunities when they appear.*

These beliefs are not slogans; they are practices she has lived out repeatedly.

When adversity appears, Mette meets it mostly head-on, but with maturity earned over time. She now pauses to consider her actions and seeks advice from a trusted network. Experience has taught her that strength includes knowing when to ask for help.

If there is one lesson she offers to others, it is this: *work out what you want in life and grab any opportunity when it presents itself. Give it a go.*

Mette Fraas Nielsen's life is not ordinary.

It is a life of courage without bravado, ambition without arrogance, and success grounded in humanity.

From a Danish farm to global boardrooms, from engineering sites to award-winning bakeries, she has shown that reinvention is not a one-time event but a lifelong skill.

Above all, her story reminds us that the most meaningful lives are often built by those willing to step forward, again and again, and say yes to what might be possible.

Peter Reitano
A Life of Service and Commitment

I had never heard of Peter Reitano when invited to review some nominations from Australian Junior Chamber (now known as JCI Australia). This was to decide on Australia's candidate for that year's Japan Academy (originally called Jaycees International Youth Voyage).

Hosted by JCI Japan, all 100+ member countries of the international young people's personal development organisation are invited to send a member with leadership aspirations. They embark on a week-long cultural, training and international experience. It was originally conducted on board a cruise ship but is now usually held in a major Japanese city. The international delegates are matched by a similar number of Japanese members. Traditionally, Australia's nominee is actually the National President-elect or is the person likely to be elected to that position in the following year.

My invitation to assess nominations had come out of the blue - many years after my age-limited active membership had ceased. This put me in a position of having no personal knowledge of the candidates and reliant on the nomination forms upon which to make my assessment.

Peter Reitano was one of three candidates - but his nomination struck me as odd. Despite being a Senator (life member of JCI – the world organisation), here was a young man based in Ingham, Queensland (where the local chapter had ceased operation some years before).

He appeared to have joined a Melbourne-based chapter to qualify for nomination. It made no sense to me as I understood that candidates should have strong local support - which appeared absent in his case.

In a vacuum of personal knowledge, I reveal publicly for the first time, that I ranked Peter's nomination last and was somewhat surprised when his nomination was successful. Obviously the other two adjudicators did have the personal knowledge that I lacked and Peter became Australia's candidate at the Japan Academy held in Kagoshima, Japan in 2009.

He went on to become Australian Junior Chamber National President in 2010 - which was a great outcome as it was to broaden his horizons and extend his contribution to the community.

I was to meet Peter for the first time nearly a decade later when we were both attending a Jaycees Biennial Reunion. We happened to have rooms on the same floor of a Tasmanian hotel which was some distance from the main function hotel. As my wife and I approached the lift, a lanky 192 cm frame loomed over us - bursting into a beaming, friendly smile when he noticed our delegate badges. He introduced himself and offered to escort us to the function hotel - commencing a great friendship and our respect for an outstanding young man committed to serving his community.

Felix Peter Reitano, affectionately known as Peter, was born into a legacy of entrepreneurship and community service in Ingham, Queensland.

He emerged as the fourth generation in a family business that spanned decades and his name traces back to a lineage of Felix's —his great-grandfather, grandfather, and father— all of whom bore the same name. To avoid confusion, Peter embraced his affectionate moniker, setting the stage for a life defined by dedicated service and a passion for making a difference.

Peter's upbringing was rooted in the tight-knit community of Ingham, where family values and a spirit of service were instilled from an early age.

He was the son of Felix John Reitano and Judith Isobel Reitano (née Whouley), whose own family history of dedication to education and community left an indelible mark on Peter's character. With five younger siblings— Christina, Angela, Robert, Michael, and Anthony—Peter grew up surrounded by love, laughter, and a sense of camaraderie that would shape his future endeavours.

Education provided Peter with a foundation for his journey ahead. Attending Gilroy Santa Maria College, he became part of only the second class to reach Grade 12 at the school—a milestone that marked the beginning of a lifelong pursuit of knowledge and personal growth.

While Peter admits that academia wasn't his strong suit, his aptitude for accounting hinted at the path he would eventually take in the family business.

As a student, Peter grappled with shyness, but beneath his reserved exterior lay a deep well of determination and a commitment to excellence. Memories of his early years evoke both joy and challenges, from cherished moments spent with cousins to the daunting task of ringing the Auction Bell at a young age—an experience that tested his introverted nature but ultimately strengthened his resolve.

Peter's professional journey began in 1988 when he joined the family business—a decision that would shape the course of his life for the next three decades.

Starting out managing the family's Indoor Cricket Centre, he transitioned to roles in furniture and real estate sales, eventually becoming a Real Estate Agent and General Auctioneer – roles that he has held for almost 30 years (over half his life). He is now one of the Directors of the family business.

Through the highs and lows of business, Peter remains steadfast in his commitment to serving customers with integrity and efficiency, carrying on the tradition established by his great-grandfather more than a century ago in 1923.

The Reitano name in their part of the world is very well known.

It is synonymous with pride, strong family values and a long-standing faithfulness to the area of Ingham and surrounds.

But Peter's impact extends far beyond the realm of commerce. Inspired by a quote from Margaret Meade, he embraces a philosophy of teamwork and community engagement, dedicating himself to making the world a better place.

His involvement with Junior Chamber International (JCI) has broadened his approach to life and community service. It awoke a spirit of adventure that has seen him travel to six of the seven continents (Antarctica being the exception) and build new friendships with JCI members throughout the world.

Despite his natural shyness, the organisation's training allowed him to be a member of a winning JCI World Debating Team at the JCI World Congress in Tunisia in 2009 and to be named as Best Speaker in that competition. He plays this down though, on the basis that he was one of the few people in that competition for whom English was their only fluent language.

Throughout his life, Peter faces adversity with resilience and grace.

He avoids confrontation by choice and is naturally unsettled when faced with adversity but overcomes this by thinking through solutions that can address the issue.

From health challenges to the devastation of a fire that consumed his family's business in 1997, he navigates obstacles with a steely resolve, emerging stronger and more determined than ever.

His dedication to community service has earned him numerous accolades.

It is no wonder that among many awards (including Australia's Centenary Medal at age 30), he was appropriately recognised as Hinchinbrook Shire's 2021 Citizen of the year when you consider the length and depth of his commitment to organisations.

These are just some to which he has contributed to for more than two decades: Ingham Maraka Festival Committee (legend award); Ingham Theatre Group; and Herbert River Crushers Rugby League (life member).

This is in addition to shorter term involvements in various capacities with Herbert River Cricket Association; Rotary Club of Herbert River (now combined with Rotary Club of Ingham to make Rotary Club of Hinchinbrook of which he has been President twice and has received a Paul Harris Fellowship); Brothers Sports & Community Club Ingham; Hinchinbrook Chamber of Commerce, Industry & Tourism of which he is currently the Vice President.

Peter is a keen sideline sports enthusiast and loves to follow cricket and rugby league.

He continued his contribution to JCI Australia as Secretary of the Australian Junior Chamber Foundation which manages the residual capital from the disposal of the organisation's Canberra secretariat building many years ago. He held that position for more than a decade until retiring from the role in 2024 and the national organisation recognised that commitment by awarding him life membership No. 9 in 2023.

Yet, for Peter, the true measure of success lies not in awards or recognition, but in the impact he makes on the lives of others.

As he reflects on his journey, Peter offers a simple yet profound lesson: do the right thing, no matter the circumstances. It's a mantra that has guided him through life's ups and downs, reminding him of the power of integrity, compassion, and unwavering determination.

In every chapter of his life—from his early days in Ingham to his adventures around the world—Peter Reitano embodies the spirit of service and adventure. As he continues to inspire others with his boundless energy and commitment to making a difference, his legacy will endure as a testament to the transformative power of community, compassion, and unwavering determination.

Bev Smith

Just Do It ... and Enjoy the Journey

Trying to recall a first meeting with someone nearly half a century ago can be problematic—especially when that contact occurs while hosting a national convention of some 750 people. Yet some impressions refuse to fade.

Bev Smith was one of those. A bright, enthusiastic young woman from country Victoria, she delivered a promotional pitch for her hometown— *"Linger longer in Yarrawonga"*— with such warmth and conviction that it lodged permanently in the memory bank. She was forthright, engaging, and unmistakably genuine. Easy to like. Easy to trust.

Our paths crossed repeatedly over the years through JCI Australia and later at international gatherings, including JCI World Congresses in Cannes, Manila, and Sapporo – the last three I was privileged to attend. Friendship grew naturally, as it often does, through shared purpose rather than deliberate design. More than twenty years after that first encounter, my wife and I found ourselves seated at the same table as Bev at the wedding of my accountant, Peta Woodard, to another JCI Australia National President, David Clark. We reminisced, laughed—and I realised how little I truly knew of Bev's full story. It is one I am grateful she has now allowed me to tell.

Some lives are mapped out with precision, guided by clearly articulated goals and timelines. Others unfold more instinctively, shaped by values, work ethic, and a deep sense of responsibility to people and place.

Bev Smith's life belongs firmly in the latter category. Hers is a story built on showing up, pitching in, and quietly doing what needs to be done—and doing it well.

Born on 11 January 1957 in Yarrawonga, Victoria, Beverley Smith—known to everyone simply as Bev—was the middle child of Wilf and Gwen Owen, arriving between older brother Wayne and younger brother Noel. Life revolved around family and the rhythms of rural living. The family farm was more than a setting; it was a classroom, a playground, and an early training ground for independence.

From a young age, Bev learned the value of being useful. Effort mattered. Contribution mattered. These were not lessons taught through lectures, but absorbed through daily example. Her parents lived their values quietly and consistently, and Bev would later emulate that same approach in her own life.

Her childhood was filled with simple pleasures—family holidays, shared work, and time spent "just doing lots of things." One early memory foreshadowed much of what was to come.

At just ten years old, Bev carefully planned a surprise birthday party for her mother. It was an early glimpse of her organisational ability, thoughtfulness, and quiet leadership—qualities that would remain constant throughout her life.

Primary school at Rennie Public School gave way to boarding at Woodstock Presbyterian Girls School in Albury—a challenging transition for a girl who had never been away from home. Boarding life was tough, the discipline stricter than anything she had known.

One incident became particularly memorable. On her birthday, in a moment of youthful high spirits, Bev threw a glass of water over a fellow student—only to be grounded by the principal for an entire term. At the time, the punishment felt excessive; in hindsight, it became a lesson in accountability and consequences. Even now, she laughs about it, understanding that lessons don't always arrive gently.

Academically, Bev was diligent and capable—studious, conscientious, and determined to do well. After her boarding years, she returned home to complete her education at Yarrawonga High School, where she thrived in a more familiar and supportive environment.

Sport played a significant role in her development. With only eighteen students at her primary school—mostly boys—team sports naturally included cricket and Australian rules football, sparking a lifelong love of both.

Athletics, however, was her standout. Bev excelled, representing her school at carnivals and discovering the confidence that comes from personal achievement.

She played every sport available, later taking up hockey, tennis and squash and continuing competitively well into adulthood. Later, even holidays were rarely sedentary, often including a few rounds of golf.

At sixteen, Bev took her first paid job at the local milk bar, working weekends. It was a modest role, but an important one—introducing her to independence, responsibility, and the satisfaction of earning her own money.

By 1975, still completing her final year of school, she demonstrated remarkable initiative. In July she typed a resume and cover letter and sent them to the only two accountants in Yarrawonga.

One replied. Bev began work as an accounting clerk just one week after finishing her Year 12 exams.

It was a simple decision, but a defining one. Bev would spend much of her working life in accounting-related roles, not driven by grand ambition, but by reliability, competence, and trust. She changed employers in 1978 but remained within the profession, working on and off over the next twenty-six years as she balanced paid employment with raising a family. Along the way, she also worked at the local golf club bistro and in other practical roles.

Work, for Bev, was never just about income—it was about contributing, learning, and doing things properly.

In March 1977, Bev married Wayne Smith.

Together they built a life firmly rooted in Yarrawonga, raising four sons and embedding themselves deeply in the community. Motherhood changed everything. Life became more precious—and at times, more frightening. Responsibility took on a deeper meaning. Decisions mattered more.

The future felt both more hopeful and more fragile.

Community involvement followed naturally. Bev had grown up watching her parents serve others without fanfare, and she absorbed that same philosophy. Service was not something you announced; it was something you did.

Wayne had been involved with the Yarrawonga Jaycees since 1977, and in time Bev formally joined, stepping into training roles from 1989. It proved to be a turning point.

Through Jaycees (JCI), her world expanded well beyond the boundaries of regional Victoria. Training programs—both in Australia and overseas—introduced her to new ideas about leadership, governance, and personal growth.

Bev discovered that she loved training. She loved helping people grow, watching confidence emerge, and seeing individuals realise their own potential. International exposure broadened her horizons and built skills she hadn't known she possessed.

These experiences eventually gave her the confidence to establish her own training and consulting business—work that felt like a natural extension of who she was: practical, people-focused, and grounded in real experience.

In 1995, Bev nominated for service on the National Board of JCI Australia. It was another step outside her comfort zone, taken without fanfare but with determination. Her willingness to say yes, to learn, and to do the work led to her election as National Vice-President in 1996 and Executive Vice President in 1997—a significant achievement and recognition of her leadership.

Despite spending years teaching others about goal-setting, Bev never fully embraced it as a personal philosophy. Life, for her, was simpler than that. If something needed to be done, she did it.

That straightforward belief—*just do it*—has underpinned every stage of her life.

It served her well when she accepted the demanding role of Practice Manager in an accounting firm. The work was relentless, but Bev thrived. She treated the business as if it were her own, applying her core principle: always do the best you can. According to her employer, she turned the practice around—no small achievement.

Three years later, as she prepared to leave Yarrawonga after fifty years, another opportunity emerged in Biloela,

Central Queensland. Once again, Bev assessed what needed fixing and quietly went about restoring stability and efficiency. No fuss. No ego. Just steady leadership.

From Queensland, life led her to Tasmania. After a short stint in the motor industry, Bev secured a role that would become her professional home for the next decade: Finance Manager of a marine biotechnology company engaged in groundbreaking seaweed research. The role combined structure with innovation—perfect for someone who valued order but welcomed new challenges. She marked ten years of service just as she prepared to take long service leave for extended travel through Europe.

In October 2011, Bev married Nick Nermut, beginning a new chapter of life and family. With Nick came three daughters, their partners, and grandchildren—expanding the family circle to fifteen grandchildren, plus step-grandchildren.

Leaving Yarrawonga had been daunting, but it opened doors to new friendships, new experiences, and a broader family than she had ever imagined.

One of the most challenging periods of Bev's life was her separation from Wayne in 2007. Although amicable, it was deeply difficult, particularly for their sons. Navigating that transition required honesty, patience, and resilience. Over time, a new normal emerged.

Today, Bev and Wayne share a respectful friendship, united by family, grandchildren, and mutual regard. Distance has never weakened those bonds.

Retirement in 2021 did not mean slowing down. Bev and Nick had already begun travelling extensively, purchasing a motorhome in Europe in 2019 and later one in Australia during the pandemic. Since then, they have spent months each year exploring Europe, while also volunteering at major Australian events such as the Birdsville Big Red Bash and the Mundi Mundi Bash.

In 2017, they completed the JCI "Grand Slam," attending multiple international conferences and World Congress in a single year—an experience that took them to places they would never otherwise have imagined visiting.

Community service remains a constant. Bev has served on countless committees and currently contributes as a member of Rotary (previously holding secretary and treasurer roles), treasurer of the Tasmanian Czech & Slovak Association, and Admin Overseer of her local Sea Rescue group—roles she finds both challenging and rewarding.

Recognition has followed, though it was never sought.

Along the way, Bev has received school awards, an Australian Jaycee Ambassador Award, a JCI Senatorship—presented unexpectedly at her 40th birthday—and a nomination for an Australian Day Award.

In quieter moments, Bev enjoys conversation, sport on television, camping, motorhome travel, knitting, crocheting, and cooking—particularly sweet dishes. She reads widely, favouring crime and forensic novels, with Dick Francis a long-time favourite. Many craft projects remain unfinished, waiting patiently.

Looking back, Bev identifies a few truths. Motherhood changed everything. JCI opened her world. Leaving home tested her courage. Each chapter brought both highs and lows, and she values them equally.

Her advice is simple: you need the downs to truly appreciate the ups. Always do your best. Be mindful of how you treat others—you never know what they are carrying.

Bev Smith's life is not extraordinary because it was easy or meticulously planned. It is extraordinary because of its consistency, generosity, and quiet strength.

She showed up. She did the work.

She served her community.

She embraced change.

And above all, she lives by one enduring belief: *"Enjoy life—you only get one chance."*

Karen Smythe

Choosing Positivity, Purpose and the Next Mission

With the passing of time, it is difficult to recall exactly when I first met Karen Smythe. I suspect it was in 1983, when I was responsible for the national public relations program for Australian Jaycees (now JCI Australia). It was a landmark year — the organisation's 50th anniversary — marked by a National Convention that drew more than 1,000 delegates and opened with a spectacular event at Sea World on Queensland's Gold Coast.

Among the many attendees was a bright, committed young member from Wilsonton Jaycees, attending her first National Convention and intent on helping promote Toowoomba's successful bid to host the event two years later. That year she would become President of the host chapter.

In time, she would go on to serve as National President and later as a JCI World Vice President.

Our paths crossed again many years later at the final three JCI World Congresses I attended — in Manila, Cannes and Sapporo. By then, Karen's reputation preceded her. It was during that period that I came to truly appreciate just how dynamic, capable and quietly influential she was, and a strong, respectful friendship developed.

So when I was encouraged to nominate to chair the JCI Australia Senate Group, it felt entirely natural to enlist Karen as my administrative right hand — overseeing some 600 JCI Senators nationwide.

It was no surprise, and a great personal delight, when she later stepped seamlessly into the role herself at the conclusion of my final term.

Yet leadership roles and international titles only tell part of the story. The question that lingered — and the one that truly matters — is this: *"what shaped the woman behind the roles?"*

Karen Smythe's story, as it turns out, began far from convention centres and world congresses, on a dairy farm outside Toowoomba, Queensland, where hard work was a daily ritual and community was woven quietly into family life.

Born on 29 June 1958 to Eric and May Folker, Karen was the eldest of three children, followed by her sister Gail in 1960 and brother Warren in 1962. The farm shaped her in ways she would not fully appreciate until much later — teaching her responsibility early, grounding her in routine, and instilling an unspoken understanding that contribution mattered.

Life on a dairy farm was demanding. Cows did not take weekends off, nor did they care about public holidays. Karen learned quickly that commitment was not something you talked about; it was something you lived. Outings were rare, money was tight, and family came first. Church was one of the few regular social activities, and the local dances — which her parents loved — were moments of lightness and connection.

Extended family often visited the farm, and Karen remembers vividly the joy of cousins arriving, her grandmother living nearby, and the sense that while they may not have had much materially, they were rich in relationships.

One of her most cherished childhood memories is learning to drive at the age of six, perched beside her father in the ute as they worked the land together. There was "a lot of kangaroo juice in the ute to start with," she recalls with humour, but also pride.

Those moments with her father were formative — teaching her confidence, independence, and trust in her own abilities long before she ever entered a classroom.

Karen attended Wyreema State School for primary education and then Harristown High School.

She enjoyed school, particularly writing, which allowed her to express herself and make sense of the world. She was the kind of student who liked things done properly and on time — a trait that would follow her throughout her life.

Like many young women of her era, however, Karen left school before completing Year 10.

The expectation then was simple: you worked. And so she did, stepping into the workforce without complaint, but with curiosity and determination.

Her early working life saw her spend 16½ years as a pharmacy assistant. It was steady, people-focused work that suited her well. She learned how to listen, how to serve, and how to remain calm in the face of pressure — skills that would later define her as a trainer and coach.

But Karen was not someone who stayed still for long. Learning had always excited her, and she continued to seek out opportunities to grow, eventually moving into a role at Heritage Building Society as a Training Officer, and later Senior Training Officer.

This was where something clicked.

Training, Karen realised, was not just about transferring knowledge. It was about unlocking potential. Helping people understand themselves, gain confidence, and step into new capability brought her a sense of fulfilment that no title ever could. That insight set her on a path that would define the rest of her working life.

Alongside her professional development, Karen became deeply involved in Junior Chamber International (JCI), joining at the age of 18. What began as a community and leadership organisation soon became a crucible for her growth. JCI exposed her to training, leadership, governance, and international perspectives far beyond anything she had known growing up on a Queensland farm. Over three decades, she would serve at every level — local, regional, state, national and international.

Karen's rise through JCI was not accidental. She worked hard, sought mentors, and listened carefully to advice — even when it was uncomfortable. She valued guidance but always took responsibility for her own decisions. This balance of humility and independence became one of her defining traits.

Her commitment to training within JCI was extraordinary.

She achieved the highest level of training internationally and spent ten years travelling the world coaching young trainers. She became State President of Queensland Junior Chamber in 1991, National President, and ultimately an International Vice President assigned to nine countries in Africa. She also held international appointments as Community Development Commissioner and Training Commissioner for Asia, roles that required not just expertise, but cultural sensitivity, adaptability, and empathy.

It was Africa, however, that changed her forever.

Serving as JCI Vice President assigned to Africa confronted Karen with realities she had never experienced. Spending nights in slum areas, seeing how people lived with almost nothing, and witnessing their resilience and joy stripped away any lingering attachment to material success.

Later, as trainer of the JCI African Academy in Kenya for six years, she visited orphanages in Nairobi where children spoke openly about being unwanted or abandoned.

Their gratitude for simple human connection left a profound imprint.

From those experiences, Karen's philosophy crystallised: material possessions mean very little. Quality of life, presence, and helping others matter far more. Today, she lives in a minimalistic apartment, content with what she needs rather than what she could accumulate. Her outlook on life shifted permanently — towards simplicity, gratitude, and purpose.

At the age of 40, drawing on decades of learning and experience, Karen took a leap of faith and started her own business, *The Vibrant Edge Pty Ltd*. It was a natural extension of everything she believed in. Through her business, she contracted to organisations across financial planning, insurance, hospitality and education, delivering both certified and non-certified training.

She became a life coach, skills coach, author, and mentor — but always, at her core, a trainer who loved helping people grow.

Her qualifications continued to expand: Certificate IV in Training and Assessment, Certificate IV in Small Business Management, Diploma in Life Coaching, advanced certification in Emergenetics, and, more recently, a Certificate in Counselling. Age, to Karen, has never been a barrier — only an invitation to the next mission.

One of her most impactful initiatives emerged when she was approached by Sports Darling Downs to help young athletes improve their public speaking and interview skills. From that conversation, *Speak Up for Sport* was born. What began as media interview and public speaking training quickly evolved into a comprehensive program covering sponsorship acquisition, social media management, goal setting, and positive mindset coaching.

Karen's philosophy was simple but powerful: athletes may have on-field coaches, but in modern sport, professionalism off-field is just as critical. Sport is a business, and young athletes need the skills to navigate it with confidence and integrity. Working face-to-face whenever possible, Karen found immense joy in watching shy teenagers transform into articulate, self-assured young professionals.

Her greatest reward, she says, has never been money. It is witnessing growth. Seeing people — whether athletes, trainers, or JCI members — achieve goals they once doubted was possible gives her an unmistakable buzz. The same feeling she experienced decades earlier in JCI, watching others rise into leadership roles, continues to fuel her work today.

Karen's life has not been without hardship.

One of her most significant challenges came when a client failed to pay, pushing her to the brink of losing both of her homes.

The experience was terrifying and humbling. She fought hard to survive financially, learning painful but invaluable lessons about due diligence, boundaries, and self-protection. Trust, she realised, must be balanced with structure. Today, her rule is clear: no deposit, no training.

Rather than allowing the experience to embitter her, Karen absorbed the lesson and moved forward — stronger, wiser, and still positive.

That positivity is not naïve. It is practised. When adversity strikes, Karen looks for the good, weighs the pros and cons, and makes decisions when the time is right. She learns, adapts, and refuses to repeat mistakes. Negativity, when it arises, is acknowledged and turned around quickly. Dwelling on the past or worrying excessively about the future has no place in her philosophy.

Life, she believes, is meant to be lived in the moment.

Outside of work, Karen's interests are as vibrant as her personality. Tennis was her sport for many years, as was golf with friends until a shoulder injury ended that enjoyment.

She is an avid reader — particularly of suspense novels and personal development books — and loves music, movies, and being a tourist in her own town.

She travels extensively and has an unexpected passion for Formula One motor racing, attending the Melbourne Grand Prix regularly and races in Singapore, Abu Dhabi and Japan.

One of her own young athletes competed in the Melbourne Grand Prix — a connection that brings her story beautifully full circle.

Community has always been central to Karen's life.

Beyond JCI, she spent decades involved in Wyreema Tennis Club, serving as secretary for many years, and Wyreema Bowling Club from the age of 12. She also gave her time as a Sunday School teacher at St John's Lutheran Church.

Recognition followed naturally, though it was never her motivation. Her awards include JCI Senator, Outstanding Senator of the World, Outstanding Appointed JCI Officer, JCI Australia Life Membership, and an Australia Day Community Award from Jondaryan Shire Council. She was also named as One of the Inspiring Jaycees of the World.

When asked about the most important lesson she would offer others, Karen does not hesitate: *"love what you are doing. Choose positivity. Learn from the negative, but do not live there."*

Perhaps the most enduring message of her life is this:

"You are never too old to have a mission."

Whether working, volunteering, or retired, there is always another way to contribute, to grow, to help. Karen Smythe's life is a testament to that belief — a reminder that an ordinary beginning can lead to an extraordinary impact when guided by purpose, resilience, and an unwavering commitment to helping others shine.

In the end, Karen's story is not about titles or accolades.

It is about choice — the choice to enjoy each day, to change when something no longer fits, and to keep saying yes to the next mission. In that way, her life stands as a quietly powerful example of what a truly *Not ORDINARY Life* looks like.

Movers & Shakers – Karen Smythe

Charity Beneficiaries

The following Charities have been nominated to receive a share of the royalties from the sale of this book by the subjects whose stories are featured in it:

Amber Community (Vic)

Australian Junior Chamber Foundation Inc.

BirdLife Australia

Breast Cancer Care (WA)

Cancer Council WA

Fly2Foundation

Free the Hounds Inc

Life Flight Australia (Darling Downs)

Mettle Women Inc.

MND Association (WA)

Red Nose Ltd (SIDS)

Royal Flying Doctor Service (Western Region)

Sea Rescue Tasmania Inc.

Hungry for more inspiring real-world stories?

**Timing is Everything:
Lessons from 21 Bold Ventures**
is your next must-read.

Success isn't just about winning or losing — it's about how you play the long game.

Through 21 captivating stories, this book takes you behind the scenes of both commercial and community projects: from a scrapped idea that turned into a $2 billion global triumph, to a derelict site reborn as a heritage attraction boosting a local economy by $40 million.

Written by an entrepreneur who's helped impact over 2 million lives, each story delivers a powerful, actionable lesson about passion, perseverance, and — most of all — timing.

You'll discover how challenges shape every journey and why true success is measured in growth, not just outcomes.

Perfect for entrepreneurs, innovators, and dreamers, *Timing is Everything* shows there's no such thing as failure — only the next bold step forward.

Don't just dream — learn, grow, and make it happen.

Obtain Your Copy Today!

Available in
- Paperback
- ePub
- PDF
- Audio

Movers & Shakers – Volume 1 | Peter J Snow OAM

More by the Author – Short Story Series

What do a business co-founder, a foster carer of 220 babies, Australia's "unluckiest" AFL player, an alpaca breeder, and a fire chief have in common? A love of a football club—and extraordinary stories of resilience and achievement.

The Tribe: Volume 1 shares 15 inspiring tales of everyday people proving greatness often lies in the ordinary. From a lolly-pop Santa to Western Australia's most decorated footballer, these diverse stories celebrate community, courage, and passion. . Introduced by someone who knows them all, this collection highlights the power of shared purpose and connection. Be inspired by their journeys and discover what extraordinary truly means

The Tribe: Volume 2 celebrates 16 more remarkable individuals connected through a football club. These inspiring stories reveal how passion, determination, and community spirit drive extraordinary achievements.

From a bush bank manager to a Serbian rugby player, a school principal, a mother of four, a CEO, a business founder, each story showcases resilience and the power of community.

Whether building careers, transforming communities, or overcoming challenges, these individuals prove greatness is within reach for us all. Be inspired by **The Tribe: Volume 2** and discover what's possible with connection and courage.

For more information on release dates, availability or contact with the Author scan the QR code at right or go to

peterjsnowauthor.com

www.ingramcontent.com/pod-product-compliance
Lightning Source LLC
LaVergne TN
LVHW021821060526
838201LV00058B/3473